How to Teach Writing Across Curriculum: Ages 6–8

Now in an updated second edition, *How to Teach Writing Across the Curriculum: Ages 6–8* provides a range of practical suggestions for teaching non-fiction writing skills and linking them to children's learning across the entire curriculum. Providing a number of suggestions for teachers and putting emphasis on creative approaches to teaching children writing in diverse and innovative ways, it offers:

- techniques for using speaking and listening, drama and games to prepare for writing;
- suggestions for the use of cross-curricular learning as a basis for writing;
- planning frameworks and 'skeletons' to promote thinking skills;
- information on key language features of non-fiction texts;
- examples of non-fiction writing;
- guidance on the process of creating writing from 'skeleton notes'.

With new hints and tips for teachers and suggestions for reflective practice, *How to Teach Writing Across the Curriculum: Ages 6–8* will equip teachers with all the skills and materials needed to create enthusiastic non-fiction writers in their primary classroom.

Sue Palmer is a writer, broadcaster and education consultant. Specialising in the teaching of literacy, she has authored over 150 books and has contributed to numerous television programmes and software packages. She is the author of *Speaking Frames: How to Teach Talk for Writing: Ages 8–10* and *Speaking Frames: How to Teach Talk for Writing: Ages 10–14*, also published by Routledge.

Also available in the Writers' Workshop Series:

How to Teach Writing Across the Curriculum: Ages 8–14
Sue Palmer
(ISBN: 978-0-415-57991-9)

How to Teach Writing Across the Curriculum: Ages 6–8

Second edition

Sue Palmer

LONDON AND NEW YORK

First edition published as *How to Teach Writing Across the Curriculum at Key Stage 1*
by David Fulton Publishers 2003

This edition published 2011
by Routledge
2 Park Square, Milton Park, Abingdon, Oxon, OX14 4RN

Simultaneously published in the USA and Canada
by Routledge
270 Madison Avenue, New York, NY 10016

Routledge is an imprint of the Taylor & Francis Group, an informa business

Typeset in Helvetica by FiSH Books
Printed and bound in Great Britain by MPG Books Group, UK

British Library Cataloguing in Publication Data
A catalogue record for this book is available from the British Library

Library of Congress Cataloging-in-Publication Data
Palmer, Sue, 1948–
How to teach writing across the curriculum : ages 6–8 / by Sue Palmer. — 2nd ed.
p. cm.
1. Language arts (Elementary)—Great Britain. 2. Language arts—Correlation with content subjects—Great Britain. 3. English language—Writing—Study and teaching (Elementary)—Great Britain.
4. Curriculum planning—Great Britain. I. Title.
LB1576.P254 2011
372.62'3—dc22

2010005853

ISBN13: 978-0-415-57990-2 (pbk)
ISBN13: 978-0-203-84600-1 (ebk)

Contents

Acknowledgements

This book owes its existence to the many teachers throughout the UK who heard about 'skeletons' on my literacy inservice courses, tried them out in the classroom and reported back. I am greatly indebted to them for their interest, enthusiasm, generosity and wisdom.

Thanks are also due to the National Literacy Strategy, which sponsored me to investigate the use of skeletons in junior classes, and David Fulton Publishers for commissioning the original books *How to Teach Writing Across the Curriculum at Key Stage 1* and *Key Stage 2.* This work made me desperately keen to know how 'skeletons' could work in the classroom with different age groups, and increased my focus on the significance of speaking and listening as a precursor of any writing activity.

The opportunity to find out more was offered by Jeremy Sugden, editor of *Child Education* magazine, who let me research and write a series of articles on using skeletons in Key Stage 1. Several of the case studies in *How to Teach Writing Across the Curriculum: Ages 6–8* are based on these articles; others have been generously provided by teachers I met during inservice travels.

I should also like to thank the children of the Abbey School, Wybourne Primary School, East Dene School, Sacred Heart Catholic Primary School, Comin Infants School, Roskear Primary School, Yew Tree Primary School and Totley Primary School for providing the many lovely examples of work. This is by far the best way of illustrating how to teach – and learn – cross-curricular writing skills.

And finally, my thanks to my current editor Bruce Roberts, who has given me the chance to update these materials, and to move beyond the restrictions placed on the original books by an educational orthodoxy that over-focused on specific literacy skills at the expense of children's natural disposition to use language for learning, and their innate capacity to build on that disposition to develop literacy.

Introduction: teaching writing

Some years ago, I was chatting with a group of primary children about the differences between talking and writing.

'Which is harder?' I asked.

They looked at me as though I was mad: 'Writing of course!'

'Why?'

There was a long silence. Then a little chap with glasses put up his hand.

'Well,' he said, choosing his words carefully. 'When you talk, you don't have to think about it. You just open your mouth and the words sort of flow out … '

He paused, his brow furrowed. 'But when you write …'

The rest of the class nodded encouragement.

'Well, you have to get a pencil, and you have to get a piece of paper, and then … and then …'

We all waited agog.

' … and then you feel really tired.'

I think that sums it up pretty well. I've been a professional writer for the last 25 years, and know exactly what he means. I go into my office, switch on the computer, the screen lights up, a new blank page sits before me, and I think … 'I'll just go and make a cup of tea.'

From speech to writing

The critical – and enormous – difference between speaking and writing is that human beings are hard-wired for speech. As long as they listen to plenty of language in their earliest years, and have opportunities to copy the sounds and words they hear, they'll start to talk. If that talk is nurtured through interaction with adults and other children, eventually the words will just flow out.

But we aren't hard-wired for literacy. Reading and writing are cultural constructs, and each new generation has to be taught how words can be turned into squiggly symbols on paper. What's more, the language of writing is very different from the natural language patterns of speech.

Speech is generally interactive – we bat words and phrases back and forth. It's produced within a shared context, so it's fragmented, disorganised and a great deal of meaning goes by on the nod. In fact, you can get by in speech without ever forming a sentence, or at least only very simple ones. To make links between ideas, speakers tend to use very simple connectives, like the ubiquitous *and* or, to denote sequence, *and then.*

Nowadays, in a world in which images are increasingly taking over from words, speech has become even less specific. Gesture, facial expression and tone of voice are often used instead of verbal description (for instance: '*And I was feeling like – Whaaat?*' where '*Whaaat?*' is pronounced in a tone of exaggerated disbelief, accompanied by an expression of wide-eyed incredulity.)

But written language is produced for an unknown, unseen audience, who may have no background knowledge at all about the subject. It must therefore be explicit and carefully crafted. It requires more extensive vocabulary than speech and organisation into sentences for clarity. The sentences become increasingly complex as the writer expresses increasingly complex ideas, using a widening range of connectives to show how these ideas relate to each other.

So the mental effort involved in writing, even for someone who's used to it, is immeasurably greater than that involved in speaking. It's not just a case of working out what you want to say without the benefit of body language, facial expression, voice tone and a shared context. You also have to translate it into a much more complex, utterly unnatural language code – different vocabulary, different sentence structures, the challenge of making a whole text hold together and make sense.

Learning to write

For apprentice writers, the task is even more complex and daunting. As well as struggling to convey meaning in an unfamiliar code, they simultaneously have to:

1. remember how words are composed of sounds, and wrestle with the exigencies of our spelling system. That means (a) applying what they know about phonics and (b) remembering which of many common English words don't actually follow phonic rules;
2. manipulate a pencil across a page, remembering how to form the letters, perhaps joining them together, leaving a space between words, and keeping the whole thing going in as straight a line as possible;
3. keep in mind all the conventions of written sentences – capital letter at the beginning, full stop at the end, other rules of punctuation, special 'written code' words.

After a lifetime as a teacher and writer, I believe that learning to write is – for the majority of children – the most complex and challenging academic task they undertake in their whole lives. What's more, despite the immense amount of mental (and physical) effort involved, the rewards in the early stages are minimal while the potential for failure is great. So it's all too easy for motivation to grind to a halt.

It's not surprising, then, that after several decades of intense effort on behalf of the teaching profession – with government initiatives and targets galore – writing is still a problem area. Children who lose motivation through repeated failure can begin to feel so 'tired' about the whole business, that they're never able to summon up the effort to become fluent writers.

Why writing is important

Yet becoming a fluent writer, even in an age of multimedia and speech-activated software, is extraordinarily important. In fact, as screen-based communication and entertainment proliferate, I believe that learning to write has become an even more critical element in the development of children's thinking skills.

As mentioned earlier, spoken language is spontaneous – you don't have to think about what you say before you say it – while written language must be carefully crafted. It requires *conscious control* on behalf of the writer. This capacity to control behaviour and thought processes is the mark of a civilised, educated brain. And increasing control of language (vocabulary, sentence structure, linking ideas together) underpins many aspects of rational thought. So, from children's first faltering efforts to spell out *The cat sat on the mat* to their ability to compose an essay at university, the act of writing helps make them more educated, civilised and rational.

Neuroscientists have found that literacy 'changes the architecture of the brain'. The human capacity for reading and writing not only allows us to record our ideas, and thus share our developing understanding of the world over time and space. It also creates massively enriched neural networks in the skulls of each and every one of us. It changes our minds.

For a young child, learning to rally all those writing sub-skills means orchestrating activity in many areas of the brain – a huge mental task (no wonder they feel tired). As their basic competence grows, the physical act of writing means children must slow down their thought processes, giving time to consider the language itself. *How can I best express this idea? How can I make the links between one idea and the next?* With ideas pinned down on a page, the writer can refine or revise them – finding links, explaining underlying connections (and perhaps exploring them further), developing arguments.

What's more, as children gradually acquire the literate vocabulary and sentence structures needed to write well, this more sophisticated language can feed into their speech, and gradually they become able to talk in literate language patterns too. Literacy is about a great deal more than reading and writing – it's about the way people think and speak and (since it helps develop self control) even how they act.

The foundations of literacy

But such a complex and important process cannot be rushed. It takes time to lay down secure neural networks, and in the early stages – as mentioned above – the learners' motivation is critical. The more I've discovered about the process of learning to write, the more convinced I am that, in the early stages, we should concentrate on laying firm foundations for all the various sub-skills involved, rather than rushing children to 'orchestrate' those skills too soon. In *Foundations of Literacy*, 3rd edition (Network Continuum, 2008) written with early years specialist Ros Bayley, I identified these as:

- competence and confidence in speaking and listening, a wide vocabulary, well-developed auditory memory and access to a range of expressive language structures;
- familiarity with the patterns of written language through frequent hearing and repeating of favourite stories, as well as sentence repetition and completion activities;
- a thorough acquaintance with the alphabet names and letters shapes;
- understanding of what writing is, what it's for and how phonic knowledge is involved in converting spoken words into printed letters;
- sound phonemic awareness and a firm understanding of the main ways speech sounds are represented in writing;
- good physical control, including hand-eye coordination, and confident manipulation of a pencil to form letter-shapes.

In order to acquire these sub-skills, children need many other activities – play and talk with other children and interested adults; songs, rhymes and opportunities to move to music; art, craft, construction and mark-making activities to hone hand-eye coordination;

and (especially for boys) plenty of active outdoor activity to develop the physical control needed to sit still in a classroom and concentrate on small-scale desk-bound work. So before we even think about getting children writing – let alone writing across the curriculum – we must make sure these foundations are well-established.

It's also much easier to learn to read than to write. Once children have learned the elements of phonics, decoding simple texts helps them internalise the sound–symbol system of English. And reading aloud helps familiarise them with the shape, rhythm and conventions of written sentences. It can also increase motivation – once children recognise the power of written language (how an authorial voice carries more weight than everyday speech), they're more prepared to make an effort to become writers themselves.

When should writing start?

In most European countries, children are not expected to pick up a pencil until they are six years old (and in the countries that do best in international comparisons of literacy scores, until they are seven). Before then, teachers concentrate on child-friendly activities to develop the sub-skills listed above. Pencils and other writing equipments are available, in writing corners and role-play areas, and most children enjoy writing as part of their play. But while their teachers encourage and support them in these emergent writing activities, there are no formal writing lessons.

In most of the UK, however, we have tended over recent decades to start children on formal writing activities at a very early age. The first edition of *How To Teach Writing Across the Curriculum* was based on the framework imposed on English schools by the National Literacy Strategy, in which whole class teaching was expected from the reception, when children are only four or five. I suspect that this tendency to rush the process has contributed to many children's long-term problems with writing, and greatly regret my part in promoting it.

But now that schools have been freed from this rigid centrally-prescribed framework, teachers should feel able to establish sound foundations for writing before beginning formal work. The 'skeleton' method of recording suggested in this book is suitable for use with children at many levels of writing readiness. As several of the case studies illustrate, skeletons can be used to organise information in pictorial form (photographs, clip art or the children's own pictures), or by manipulating sentences scribed by the teacher.

This means the sub-skills of 'organizing ideas' may be taught alongside phonemic awareness, phonic knowledge, the skills underpinning handwriting and all the other foundations of literacy. Using skeletons to record activities and discoveries also provides many opportunities for purposeful talk and vocabulary development. And fluent confident spoken language is probably the most important foundation of all, not only for literacy but for learning in general.

In a school where teachers have taken the time and effort to build solid foundations in this way, by the time children are six or seven years of age they should be ready to take conscious control of their own thought processes. And to make the momentous leap from the spontaneous natural language of speech to conscious manipulation of the complex symbolic system we know as 'writing'.

PART 1

The two horses model for cross-curricular writing

You can't teach children to write before they can talk. It's putting the cart before the horse.

It's over a decade now since a teacher in Yorkshire uttered those words at one of my inservice courses. As I drove home that night I started wondering exactly how teachers could ensure that the 'horse' of talk was properly hitched up to draw the 'cart' of writing.

Eventually, after long conversations with many colleagues (especially my fellow literacy consultant Pie Corbett), I concluded that, in order to write, children need two sorts of talk:

- talk for learning – plenty of opportunities to use the simple spontaneous language of speech to ensure they understand the ideas and content they're going to write about;
- talk for writing – opportunities to meet and internalise the relevant patterns of 'literate language', to help them turn that content into well-crafted sentences.

So children need not one but two 'horses' to draw the writing 'cart':

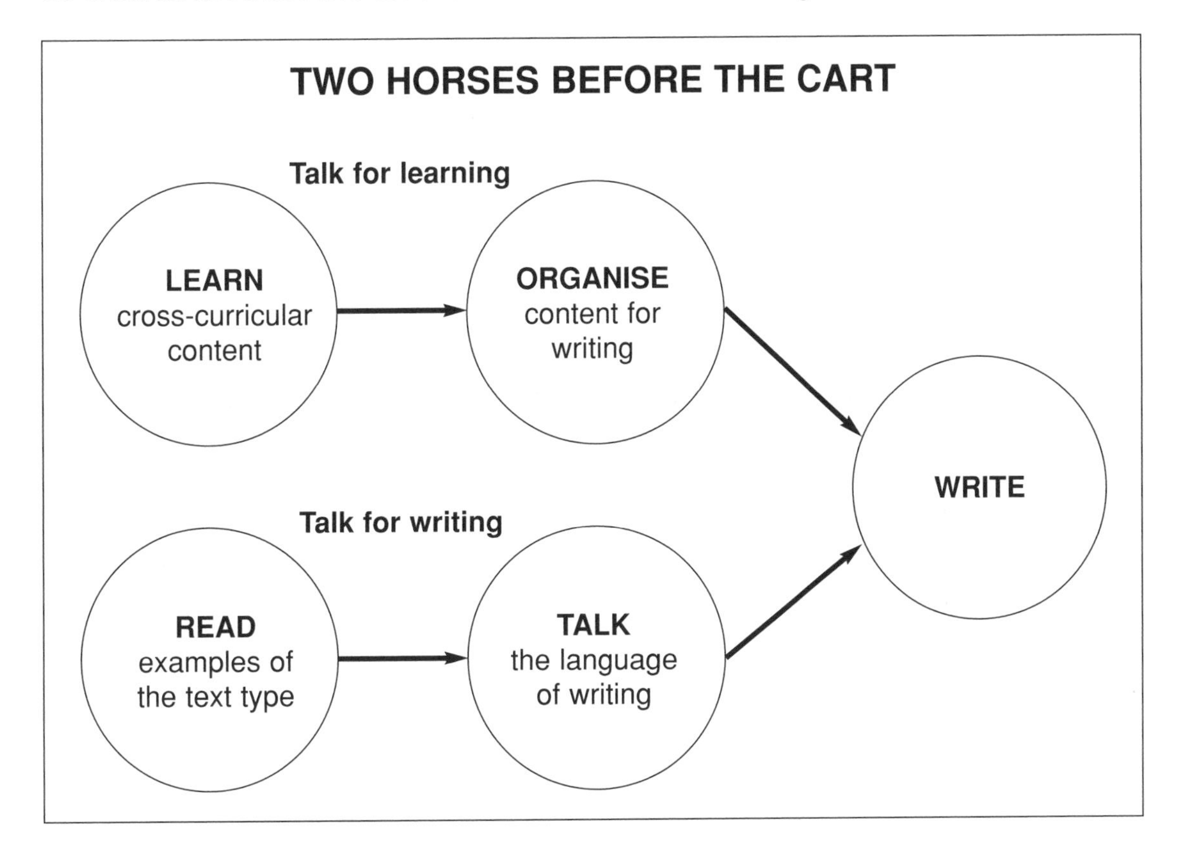

Figure 1.1 A teaching plan for cross-curricular literacy (simple form)

1.1 Talk for learning

Learn cross-curricular content

In order to understand the content of cross-curricular teaching, young children need – just as they have always needed – plenty of opportunities for talk. These are provided through the sort of good infant practice long recognized as valuable opportunities for activity and interaction, such as:

- learning corners and role-play areas, preferably linked to the subject-matter concerned, in which they can engage in imaginative play (this may sometimes be enhanced by adult involvement in the children's play, expanding vocabulary and ideas);
- outings, excursions, visits and other opportunities to find out about the wider world through experience and talk to a range of adults;
- active engagement in learning whenever possible: making, doing, experimenting, learning through play;
- plenty of 'props and prompts' for learning – for instance, relevant items to look at, touch and talk about while you are teaching or sharing a text, and opportunities for 'Show and Tell';
- opportunities to 'experience' factual information with the teacher's direction in drama lessons and through specific drama activities like hot-seating;
- using puppets to act out what they have learned, and to 'speak through' when explaining something (shy children often find it much easier to talk to a puppet or soft toy than to the class, and may also be able to respond on a puppet's behalf when they find it difficult to speak up themselves);
- storytelling sessions – listening to adults telling stories, which can of course be true stories, and having opportunities to tell them themselves;
- responding to ideas through music, movement, art and craft.

Without such opportunities for active, motivating learning, young children are unlikely to develop the ideas, concepts, vocabulary and excitement about what they have learned that underpins good writing. With so much attention these days to 'pencil and paper' work it is sometimes tempting to think that this type of practice is a waste of valuable time. In fact, it is the bedrock of literacy.

Experience has shown that certain speaking and listening activities sit particularly comfortably with the different text types we use for cross-curricular writing, as shown in the boxes. These activities reflect the underlying structures of thought upon which the text types depend, and thus link to the planning skeletons described in the next section.

Recount content

Before writing recounts children should be clear on the details and sequence of the story through activities such as:

Retelling: select children to retell short sections of the story to the class. Or ask children in pairs to retell it to each other.

Role-play: ask children in pairs or groups to dramatize significant sections of the story, which they can then re-enact for the class.

Teacher in role: take on the role of a key character in the story yourself, and draw the class with you in re-enacting the story.

Puppetry: let children act out the story with puppets. They can improvise lines as they go, or one child can be narrator, telling the story while the puppets perform.

Freeze-frame: ask groups of children to create living tableaux of incidents in the story. Invite participants to step out of each tableau, and comment on what's going on and their part in it.

Instruction content

The best way to familiarise oneself with the content of instructions is actually to carry out the process (or, if that's not possible, watch it), talking it through as you go.

Partnered work: ask children to carry out the process (or watch it being carried out) in pairs, stopping after each stage to talk through exactly what has been done.

TV demonstration: ask pairs or groups to give a demonstration of the process, describing what they're doing, as if they were the presenter on a TV programme. Others watch and question as necessary.

Running commentary: ask pairs or groups to mime the process (e.g. Road Safety Rules), or act it out with puppets, while others give a running commentary – like a road safety public service broadcast.

Barrier game: this is a good way for children to find out whether their instructions are clear enough. Give two children the equipment needed for an activity (e.g. a potato and some Mr Potato Head pieces), place a screen between them so neither can see what the other's doing. One child decides on the activity and carries it out, giving instructions as s/he goes, so the other can mimic it. Remove the barrier and check how successful the instructions were.

Report content

Non-chronological reports involve accurate and clear description. The traditional **'Show and Tell'** is the starting point for this, but you could also use activities like these:

Tell Mr Bear: Mr Bear knows absolutely nothing. Ask children in pairs to work out a clear description of the item/topic in question that will ensure his complete understanding.

Visiting alien: you play an alien visitor to Earth, totally ignorant about humans, their ways and possessions. Give individual children pictures of earth objects (e.g. a pillar box, a car, a bed) and ask them to explain their function to the alien. The rest of the group can chip in to help if necessary.

Brains Trust: when children have found out information on a topic, create a Brains Trust panel so each can give a brief talk to the class on their subject then answer questions.

TV documentary/newscast: as in the case study on the previous page – this could include commentary, interviews and, where appropriate, mini-dramatisations.

Barrier game: give one child a simple picture or artefact related to the topic and place a screen between them so the other child can't see it. The first child must describe the item so that the second can draw it, or pick out a duplicate from a given selection. (When using barrier games to practise description, illustrated wrapping paper – e.g. paper with lots of pictures of cats – can be useful. Give the first child a cut-out of one cat, and the second a complete sheet to spot the appropriate cat.)

Another aspect of non-chronological report writing is the development of categorisation skills:

Sorting activities: most infant classrooms have games or activities requiring children to sort items into groups, e.g. model animals, coloured shapes, pictures of activities. Provide items of this sort related to cross-curricular work, ask pupils in pairs to sort them into groups and then explain the reasons behind their choices.

In the hoop: lay a number of hoops on the ground to represent different categories of information in your current project (e.g. fruit, dairy products, meat, vegetables). Ask each pupil to complete a sentence (e.g. 'A .... is a type of ....') and go to stand in the correct hoop.

The corner game: choose four categories related to your topic, and make signs to put in the four corners of the hall to indicate the categories. On slips of paper write words or phrases, or draw pictures, which fit into one or other of the categories. Children take a slip and read it, then run around the hall until a given signal, such as a whistle, when they must rush to the appropriate corner. Each child (or selected children) then explain their presence in their particular corner: 'My paper says __________. I came to the__________ corner because________'

Explanation content

The best way to familiarise children with scientific concepts such as cause and effect is through involving them in meaningful activities, followed by discussion. Other preliminary activities could involve:

Physical theatre: think up a way to dramatise the process, changing children into caterpillars that turn into butterflies, bones/muscles in an arm, seeds that grow, etc.. Pairs or groups mime the process, while others give a commentary.

Teacher (or puppet) in role: you (or the puppet) act the part of an earnest but very dim seeker after knowledge, requiring the clearest of clear explanations.

Organise content for learning

During the early years of primary education, children are likely to meet many examples of four major non-fiction text types. They may also need to record cross-curricular learning that fits these structures:

- **recounts** (see page 42);
- non-chronological **reports** (see page 48);
- **instructions** (see page 55);
- simple **explanation** texts (see page 61).

They may also come across the remaining two key text types – **persuasion** and balanced **discussion** – but seldom need to write or record this information. So this section and the case studies that follow deal only with the four listed above.

The different text types are characterised by their underlying structures – the way that particular types of information are organised for writing. Awareness of these structures can become a powerful aid to planning, allowing children to organise their ideas and understanding in the form of notes or pictures before – or, especially in the early stages, **instead of** – writing.

Skeletons for writing

I originally devised the 'skeleton' frameworks shown in the box for the English National Literacy Strategy. At the time, we called them 'graphic organisers' or 'diagrammatic representations', neither of which were snappy titles to use with young children. It was a little boy in the north east of England who christened them. He rushed up to his teacher with the words: 'They're skeletons, aren't they, Miss? They're the skeletons that you hang the writing on!' Thanks to that unknown Geordie lad, the skeleton frameworks became instantly memorable.

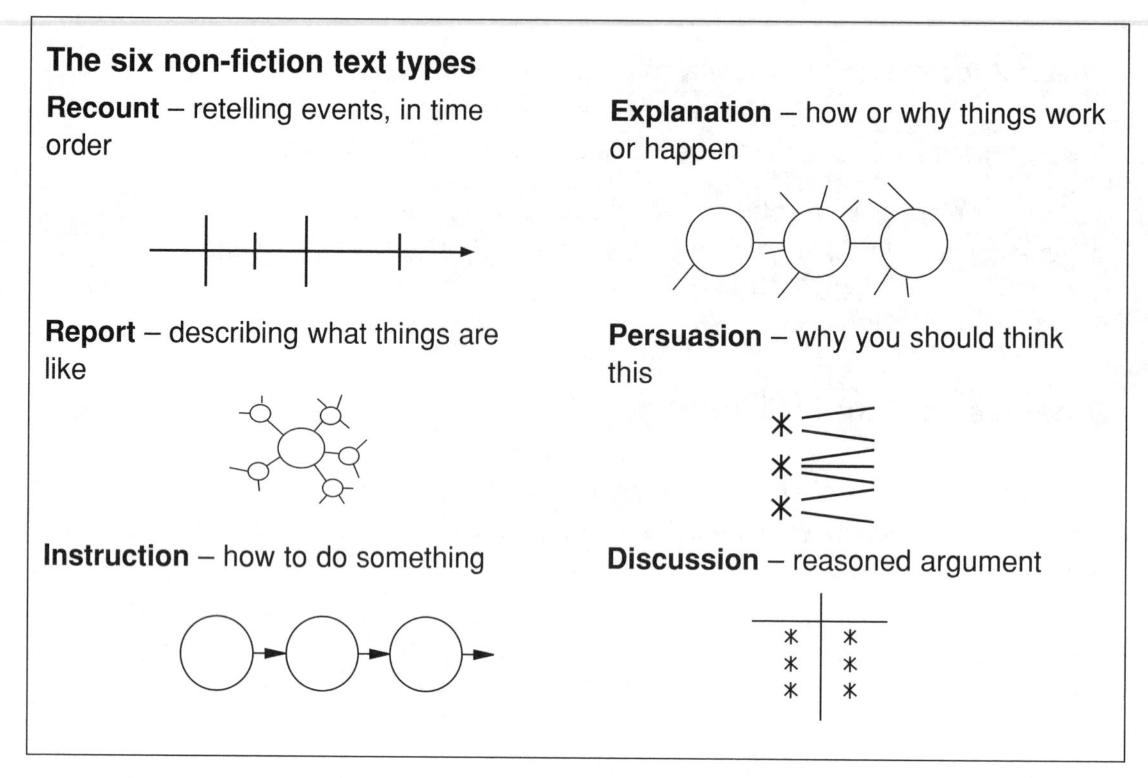

Figure 1.1.1 A range of skeletons

They were originally devised for older primary children, but extensive work by teachers across the UK has shown that skeleton planning frameworks can also be used very effectively by younger children.

A range of skeletons

The skeleton frameworks shown above are intended to be representative of each of the text types. As such they provide a visual 'icon' which reminds children of the structure of the text:

- a **timeline** icon was chosen to represent recount because it is a simple, clear indicator of chronological order (using left → right as an indicator of time passing), and visually easy to remember;
- the **simple flowchart** icon for instructions demonstrates sequence in the same way, but the circles suggest a number of discrete steps or stages in the process;
- in contrast, the **spidergram** icon shows clearly that chronology is not involved in writing report text: here the visual display suggests a basic central concept that radiates information organised into categories;
- the **complex flowchart** icon indicates that explanations are usually sequential but that there is further contributory detail at each stage: here the sequence involves cause and effect;
- the **pronged bullet** icon for persuasive writing suggests that the key to organisation is the arranging of arguments into a number of major points, each of which requires elaboration in the form of evidence or further background information;

- a **for-and-against grid** suggests that discussion text involves the organisation of points + elaboration on both sides of an argument.

Experience suggests that it is best to use the particular skeleton icon as a planning framework when introducing a particular text type, to help children internalise the underlying structure. However, there are many other ways in which each text type might be represented, and children should also be encouraged to recognise these and choose the one that best suits any individual occasion:

- the sequential, chronological structure of **recount** and **instructions** could be represented by a story-board, a flow chart, a calendar or clock face diagram, or simply a numbered list;
- a very simple **report** might be better represented by a labelled picture or diagram; comparative reports often require a grid skeleton;
- **explanation** text sometimes requires multiple cause–effect boxes or a cyclical structure (see page 61), or may sometimes be represented by a diagram or sequence of diagrams – in fact, creating graphic representations of the structures underlying individual explanation texts is an excellent way of helping children develop their understanding of cause and effect.

As children become familiar with the idea of skeletons, their repertoire of graphic representations can be gradually enlarged.

How to use skeletons

Skeleton planning provides a link between cross-curricular content and specific teaching of writing skills. Teachers can introduce children to these ways of organising ideas by:

- demonstrating how to use skeletons themselves as simple note-taking devices and aides-memoire throughout the curriculum;
- teaching children how to draw the skeletons, and recognise which sorts of ideas and writing are associated with each skeleton;
- using skeletons to link knowledge and understanding acquired in a wide range of subject areas with the literacy skills required to record that understanding.

If, for instance, the literacy teaching objective for the week is recount writing, content can be selected from anywhere in the curriculum – perhaps a story from history or a recent activity or outing. The children can help to organise these facts onto a timeline, in the form of brief notes (odd words or phrases), or even pictures.

Debbie Billard, then a teacher in Rotherham, coined the term 'memory-joggers' for these notes. She explains to the children that memory-joggers are not proper sentences – just anything that will jog the class's memory when they come to write.

This timeline can be used like a carrier bag to bring this cross-curricular content to the literacy lesson. Once children have been taught the relevant language features of recount text, they can use their memory-joggers to write. Debbie's suggestion is to 'turn your memory-joggers into sentences'.

Most of the suggestions for using skeletons at Key Stage 1 have been provided by teachers who, like Debbie Billard, used them as a planning device for teaching cross-curricular writing to their classes. A selection of case studies is included in Part 2, each providing new insights into the teaching process.

Teachers who have used skeleton frameworks with their classes have pointed out a number of advantages:

- making skeleton notes helps children organise what they have learned to aid memorisation of the facts;
- many children (especially boys) find it helpful to make this kind of 'big picture' record, so they have an overview of the whole piece of writing before beginning to write (which is, by its nature, a linear sequential process, rather than a holistic one);
- today's children are highly visually literate and skeleton planning helps them use visual memory skills to aid learning;
- as children learn a repertoire of skeletons, they can use them to take notes for a variety of purposes, not just as a precursor to writing;
- skeletons allow teachers and children to make clear links between literacy skills and the rest of the curriculum;
- planning on a skeleton allows children to organise the content of their writing in advance (including dividing material into sections and paragraphing) – it means that when they actually settle down to write, they can concentrate entirely on the language of writing;
- making a skeleton with the class provides an opportunity for highly focused speaking and listening;
- making a skeleton with a partner is a good focus for paired talk;
- using skeletons develops children's thinking skills.

It seems clear from talking to teachers that skeletons have the potential to be more than simple planning devices for writing. Perhaps the most exciting suggestion is that skeleton planning can become a way of developing generic thinking skills – helping children recognise the different ways human beings organise their ideas, depending on the subject matter we're addressing. In the case studies on pages 18–39, teachers have shown that, through using these visual models, even very young children can grapple with the structures that underlie thought and language.

1.2 Talk for writing

Once pupils have grasped the content they are to write about, they need help in acquiring appropriate language structures to express it. As is shown on pages 42, 48, 55 and 61, each of the four text types covered in Key Stage 1 are characterised by certain language features.

It isn't helpful for young children to go into grammatical details of these language features. Personally, I think it best just to use any essential grammatical vocabulary in context and hope they pick it up, rather than try to 'teach' it. (I once watched a Finnish kindergarten teacher doing a quick circle time with a handful of three-year-olds and saying 'My sentence today is: *My name is Elke.*' Each child then said the sentence, completing it with their own names. It occurred to me that, if they did a sentence completion task like that several times a week for three years, and it was always preceded by the words 'My sentence today is…', no one would ever have to teach them the meaning of 'sentence'.)

By Year 2 (Primary 3) certain grammatical terms, such as 'verb' and 'noun' can be helpful to allow generalisations about spelling and other writing conventions, e.g. 'When you're writing about the past, a lot of verbs end in –ed' (see Appendix 1). But it's much more important that children become increasingly familiar with the sorts of words, phrases and sentence structures associated with common types of writing.

Read examples of the text type

Reading, in any aspect of literacy, should always precede writing. Every teacher knows that children who read a lot of stories for pleasure tend also to be good at writing stories – they absorb the rhythms and patterns of narrative language through repeated exposure. They also pick up new vocabulary by meeting it in context. Nowadays however, with the ready availability of screen-based entertainment, fewer children see the point of reading for pleasure, so fewer of them tend to be 'natural' story writers.

This has, in fact, always been the case with non-fiction writing, particularly in the early stages of literacy. The non-fiction text types described in the previous part have various textual characteristics with which writers need to be familiar. But since most reading materials in the early stages of primary school tend to be fiction, few children have any great familiarity with them.

So it's worth going back to first principles and working out how children acquire new forms of language from their earliest days. If we then apply these principles to the acquisition of 'literate language' patterns, perhaps we can compensate for lack of experience in reading. (And if we're really lucky, perhaps our efforts can turn some children onto more reading for themselves, too.)

Listen > imitate > innovate > invent

Babies learn to speak by **listening** to the adults around them, and **imitating** the sounds they hear. This involves tuning into the phonemes of the language, and much baby babble is practise of these individual sounds – bababaaba, dadadada, gagagaga, and so on. But they also imitate the patterns and rhythms of speech, babbling away in response to adult language, so it often sounds as if they're joining in the conversation with their nonsense talk. As babies and toddlers are exposed to more and more spoken language, they start picking up whole words and phrases and imitating them. Gradually, through the miracle of human language acquisition, they work out how to **innovate** on the language patterns they hear, and finally **invent** whole speeches for themselves.

Children from educated homes are also frequently exposed to 'literate language' patterns, partly because their parents read to them a lot, but also because the adult language going on around them day-by-day is pretty literate too. These children are at a huge advantage when they come to school, because they're already familiar with the vocabulary and language structures of writing. But teachers can ensure that all children in the class get as many opportunities as possible to listen, imitate, innovate and invent along literate lines – and if nursery teachers can also be persuaded of the value of such activities, perhaps we could start to level the playing field a little for children from disadvantaged backgrounds.

Reading aloud to children

The most obvious way to expose all children to literate language patterns is to read aloud to them as often as possible. In *You Can Teach Your Class To Listen* (Scholastic) I suggest using the RA-RA-RA technique (Read Aloud, Read Along, Read Alone) with young children. Through repeated listening to a picture book, they begin to join in (imitating the reader), and gradually recite large chunks, or even the whole, of the book.

RA-RA-RA

Make a collection of picture books suitable for RA-RA-RA and, as you introduce them to the children, keep them in a special RA-RA-RA box. They should be enjoyable 'quick reads' with repetitive, rhythmic or patterned language. From the beginning, include non-fiction books along with storybooks.

Have daily Read Aloud sessions when you read:

- the Book of the Week (a featured picture book that you read every day to build up children's familiarity);
- one other book with which the children are already familiar;
- one book requested by the children.

With young children, you might have two or three Read Aloud sessions scattered through the day, each fairly short. As you build children's listening stamina, you might prefer to move towards one main session. Don't attempt to 'teach reading' in these sessions – make your main aims:

- to have fun and develop children's interest and delight in sharing books you read aloud;
- to encourage them to read along and, gradually, to hand the 'reading' over to the children so they 'read' alone.

Buy duplicate copies of your RA-RA-RA books (if possible a few of each title) for children to take home and share with parents. Explain the principles of RA-RA-RA to parents so they – and other adults – can share books in the same way at home.

Even when children can read for themselves, it's important to keep reading aloud to them. There should be at least one 'booktime' session in every classroom, every day – and remember to include good non-fiction as well as fiction. Take other opportunities to read non-fiction texts aloud to children as part of your work across the curriculum, to familiarise them with the vocabulary and language patterns of the text types they'll one day be expected to write.

Children reading aloud

In recent years, there's been a considerable decrease in the amount of time children spend reading aloud. While I wouldn't advocate a return to teachers 'hearing the reading' for hours on end, I think we should reconsider the importance of children's own oral reading.

As an opportunity to imitate literate language patterns, reading aloud has much to offer. It gives children the chance to hear literate language patterns produced from their own mouths; to know how standard English and sophisticated vocabulary *feels*; to respond physically to the ebb and flow of well-constructed sentences, learning incidentally how punctuation guides meaning and expression. There's a pay-off to be had in both speech and writing when we let accomplished authors put words into our pupils' mouths.

So, instead of scorning the old idea of 'reading round the group', I think we should look for ways to re-establish it – not necessarily to the teacher during guided reading, but perhaps to a classroom assistant, a parent helper or a tape-recorder. We should also be looking throughout the curriculum for other opportunities for children to read decent texts aloud, and encouraging other rhetorical exercises – reciting poetry, learning scripts for plays, declaiming speeches.

One of the best ways to ensure oral reading practice for all children is **paired reading**, when two children share a book or short text, dividing the reading between them. Depending on their level of ability, this could be alternate pages or alternate paragraphs. For younger children and those with special needs in literacy, reading alternate sentences works well – and encourages them to look for the full stops, and thus take note of sentence boundaries.

As well as regularly sharing storybooks in pairs (which is an excellent way of keeping the rest of the class productively engaged while the teacher works with a group), pairs of children can be given non-fiction texts linked to cross-curricular work to read aloud together. When the class needs some subject knowledge, paired reading of a text is a good way to provide it.

Talk the language of writing

Speaking frames

We can also provide opportunities for children to innovate on written language patterns, by creating 'speaking frames' for the sorts of sentence structures they're expected to produce in their writing.

- **Listen**: children hear examples from exemplar texts read aloud, e.g. clear, concise introductory sentences in an autobiographical recount: '*My name is Jessica Martin and I am six years old. I live in Manchester with my mum and my little brother Baz.*'
- **Imitate**: children familiarise themselves with the language patterns as they read the exemplar text aloud themselves.
- **Innovate**: children think of information related to themselves which could fit into a 'speaking frame' based on the examples:

  My name is ____________ and I am ____ years old. I live in ____________ with ______________.

- **Invent**: once familiar with a construction, children should be able to use it – and adapt it – in various ways in their own speech and writing.

Often we expect children to go straight to the 'inventing' stage in writing with little or no opportunity to internalise language structures through the experiences of the earlier stages. It is therefore worth looking for ways to integrate the **listen > imitate > innovate > invent** sequence into day-by-day teaching, to familiarise children with written language patterns (including sentence constructions), and to allow them the experience of producing, from their own mouths, more sophisticated language than they would usually use.

The innovation stage, using a 'speaking frame', can be a regular part of shared work. More able children should try 'filling in' the speaking frame first, so that the less able have the opportunity to hear it several times before it comes to their turn. After half a dozen or so children have had a go, so that everyone is comfortable with the construction, everyone can be asked to 'fill in' the speaking frame for their partner. (More able children could be given the task of conveying the same information in different words.)

Speaking frames can be devised for any sort of language use, including practising the use of connectives, voicing opinions, and rehearsing sentence structures for comparison, contrast, cause and effect, etc..

Sentence level work

As mentioned above, novice writers have enough on their plates orchestrating phonics, sentence structure, content and handwriting without having to worry about grammar as well. Sentence level teaching should be very light-touch, and – as far as possible – should engage children in active investigation of language.

This usually begins with **shared reading** of examples of a particular text type and talk about how authors express their ideas. Children can then be sent off to collect examples of the sorts of language they use from other similar texts, e.g.:

- time connectives in recount;
- imperative ('bossy') verbs in instructions;
- the use of examples in report;
- causal language structures in explanation.

Once children are able to write, they can be alerted to grammatical patterns through:

- oral games, e.g. changing verbs into the past tense;
- class collections of words and phrases (e.g. posters for time connectives or cause-and-effect words; banks of useful adjectives – 'words for big', 'words for little', etc.);
- focused speaking and listening activities in which children create sentences of their own, featuring the appropriate language features (e.g. see Speaking frames, above)
- see also Appendix 1: Grammar (page 84).

The key to all these activities is plenty of opportunity for all children to be actively engaged, especially in speaking and listening. Sometimes it's possible to do this as a class, but more often the solution is paired work.

Paired work

Each child is allocated a 'talking partner' – someone with whom they can be trusted to work well. Whenever the opportunity arises you say: 'Turn to your partner. You have 30 seconds [or two minutes, or whatever] to discuss....' Selected pairs can then retell their deliberations to the class.

Teachers who have used this system effectively stress the importance of training and careful organisation.

- Most children need considerable training to do it well. One child works as the teacher's partner to model the appropriate behaviour, then the group splits into pairs to try it. There should also be opportunities for the group to discuss the point of the exercise, and good and bad points of procedure.
- Where there's a teaching assistant in the class, the teacher and assistant can model a paired discussion before asking the children to try it.
- Snippets from training videos can also be useful for showing the class how the system works. The short 'Taking a closer look' section at the end of 'Scooters' on the old NLS video *Developing Early Writing* video is a good example.
- Children should be suitably paired. Most teachers find ability pairings work best, but obviously this varies depending on the children. Pairs should be reviewed frequently to check that the children are still happy working together.
- Pupils should automatically sit next to their partner for literacy – when gathering for shared work, it helps to have marks on the floor (e.g. carpet squares) in the literacy corner.
- It also helps to have posters on the wall as reminders of routines (see on next page).

Talking partners can also double as 'writing partners', allowing children to take advantage of oral rehearsal and oral revision of their work. The following technique can be rehearsed during shared work, then integrated into Paired Writing activities:

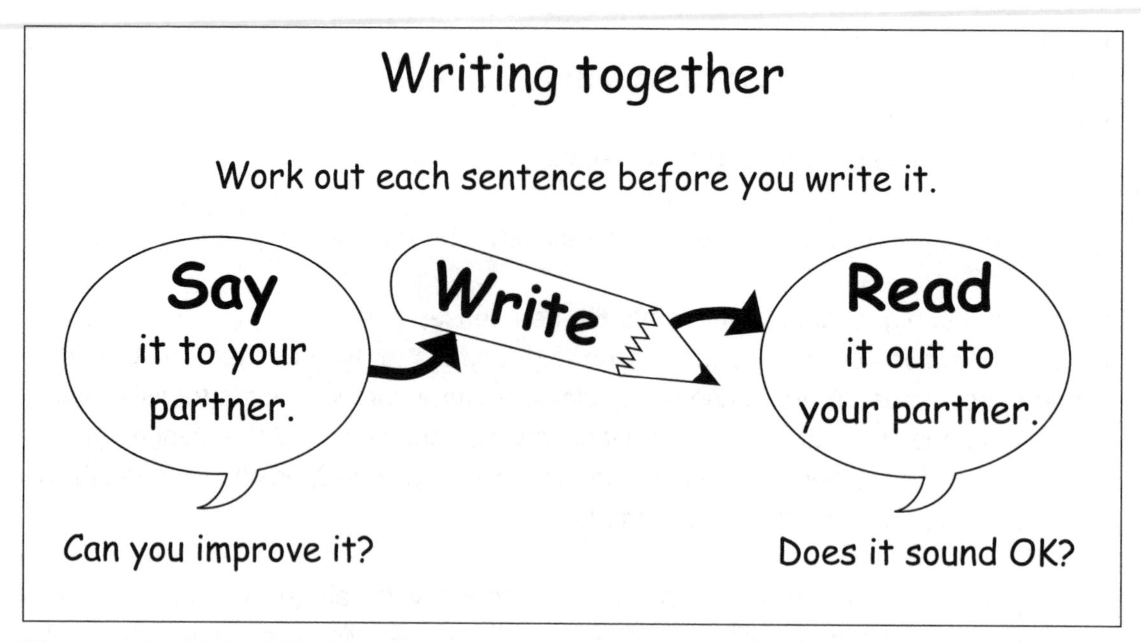

Figure 1.2.1 Paired Writing poster

Activities of this kind may seem time-consuming, but in the long run, children's literacy development is likely to be accelerated by increased opportunities for structured, directed speaking and listening.

Oral rehearsal of each sentence (or in longer sentences, each clause) helps children:

- think of the idea they are expressing as a whole;
- check that what they are about to write makes sense;
- remember what they are writing as they tussle with the problems of transcription;
- have guidance as to how the writing will 'sound'.

The routine below, devised by a teacher in Bolton, sums it up the stages in composition admirably. Teachers can demonstrate this procedure themselves in Shared Writing, and encourage children to use it during independent work.

Figure 1.2.2 Oral rehearsal poster

Our 'two horses' model for cross-curricular writing now looks like this:

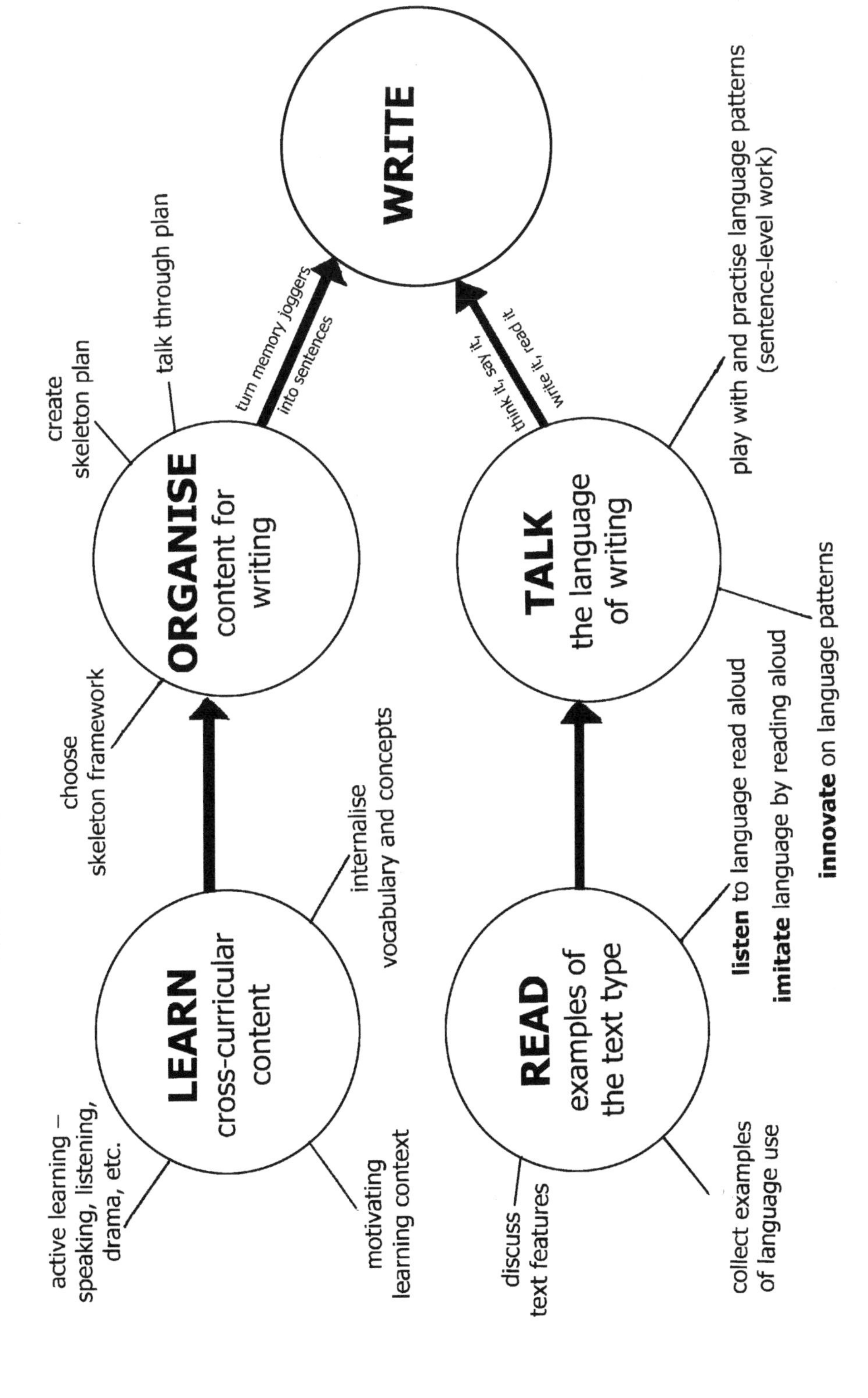

Figure 1.2.3 A teaching plan for cross-curricular writing (expanded form)

PART 2

Case studies

2.1 Recount writing

From the very earliest stages, we can use pictures or simple words on timelines to help children recognise time order, and use it to recall specific events. A timeline can provide a useful focus for highly directed speaking and listening activities.

Case study 1: our day at school

Maggie Greenhalgh, Headteacher of The Abbey School, Glastonbury, made a timeline with seven nursery children, all four years old. She talked with the children about what they do at school, and then asked them to choose an aspect of the day to draw. Maggie pinned up a timeline along the wall and the children chose the order to put the pictures along it. She reported that, all in all, their ability to sequence their daily activities was extremely good, and the exercise was a 'useful way to develop thinking skills, as well as beginning the continuum of teaching for recount writing'.

Having introduced the idea, Maggie could see many other ways of using timelines with this age group, to help improve children's appreciation of chronological order in preparation for writing when they were older. She intended to make two timelines of the trip the class would be going on in a week's time:

- one before, to use as a focus for talking about the trip in advance, and to help children think about it and give them a framework of events to expect;
- one after, to help them recall and record what happened.

It is now relatively easy to record actual events as they happen, using a digital camera. Photographs can be used to create a timeline, and to provide a motivating focus for children's talk before writing.

Figure 2.1.1 Picture timeline of a school day, by nursery children at The Abbey School, Glastonbury.

Case study 2: the wedding

Tara Chappell and Anne Hulley of Wybourn Primary School, Sheffield, used photographs as part of an R.E. project about 'weddings', in which six-year-old children created a wedding planner portfolio for a member of staff about to be married. After a number of other activities involving writing in a variety of non-fiction genres, the class staged their own wedding with children taking the parts of the bride, groom, vicar, guests and so on. The ceremony was videoed and photographed (just like a real wedding), and these records provided a visual record of the event when the class came to write about it.

Watching the ceremony on video provided many opportunities for animated talk about their wedding, after which the pupils were well-equipped to organise a sequence of photographs to retell the events in chronological order. The teachers used these for Shared Writing, over a number of short sessions. Each provided an opportunity to emphasise one aspect of recount writing, as well as revision of other word and sentence level teaching.

In session 1, the teacher gave a demonstration of how to convey the information in the picture as two sentences, both in the past tense:

> 'Now, what happened in this photo? Who was waiting at the ceremony? Yes, the groom waited at the end of the aisle. I'll write that sentence: *The groom waited at the end of the aisle.* I'll do another sentence to say something about what the groom looked like. Now, I need to remember to start my sentence with a capital letter. *He was wearing a very smart black suit with a flower in his button hole.* I wonder, how do I write *flower*? I'll say it slowly and stretch it out. How many sounds are there? f-l-ow-er – four. There!'

The children then wrote their own sentences to describe what was happening in the picture. In session 2, the class decided on another sentence for the teacher to scribe:

The bride and bridesmaids came down the aisle:

> 'Let's start with a word to show the order things happened. Look at the list of time starters we made – *after that, next, in a while, suddenly, all of a sudden, then, straight after that* ... Which connective can we start our new sentence with? Turn to your partners and make up your sentence starting with a time starter ...
>
> I'm going to use Nicola's idea because I like the way she used *in a while* from our list, and the word *walked.*'

Pupils in pairs then looked at the next picture in the sequence (the ceremony) and composed a sentence about it, beginning with a time connective. They wrote this on their individual white boards. For independent work, pupils wrote about the next picture in the sequence. In the third session, the recount was completed, using the same technique.

Case study 3: Grace Darling

Debbie Billard at East Dene School in Rotherham introduced the use of timeline skeletons to her class of six- and seven-year-olds, as part of their project on the seaside. To familiarise them with the concept, she read them a recount about heroism at sea – the story of Tom Bowker (see Appendix 3, p. 93). Although this was a demanding passage for Year 2, the children liked the story, and it inspired plenty of discussion – talking about the unusual words and asking 'why' questions about what happened. She then showed how to put the main events on to a timeline.

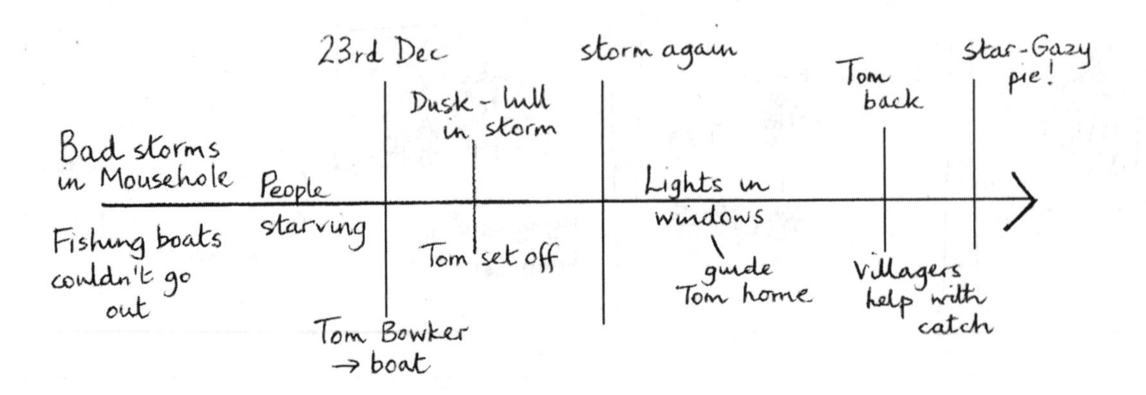

Figure 2.1.2 Diagram of Tom Bowker story

The children took to the idea of this visual representation very easily, which Debbie felt reflected a high level of visual literacy, due to their familiarity with TV and computers: 'Today's children are very comfortable with this type of visual display, and I think we should make use of that in developing literacy skills.'

Meanwhile, the class was involved in a history topic on Grace Darling. This featured another story of heroism at sea, which Debbie told to the children, reinforcing their understanding by the use of drama (freeze-framing), role play (hot-seating) and artwork. Once the children were familiar with the events, they were enthusiastic about helping to put them on a timeline. Debbie demonstrated how to reduce the key details of the story to 'memory-joggers' (words, phrases or little pictures – whatever would best help them remember the details when they came to write). She preferred the term 'memory-joggers' because it was more meaningful to them than the conventional term 'notes'.

She then gave the class a free choice of how to make their own timeline models of the Grace Darling story. Some did it completely in pictures, some used a mixture of pictures and labels. 'I watched one boy carefully draw a series of circles across a strip of paper, number them, then draw a captioned picture in each. I think it's really important that children should make their own decisions about how to present information – it gives them confidence and ownership of the content. Even the less able children could record their understanding in this way, and then talk through the story with a partner.'

Next she showed how to plan an introduction to set the scene for readers by answering some key questions:

- Who is the story about?
- What did she do?
- Where did it happen?
- When did it happen?

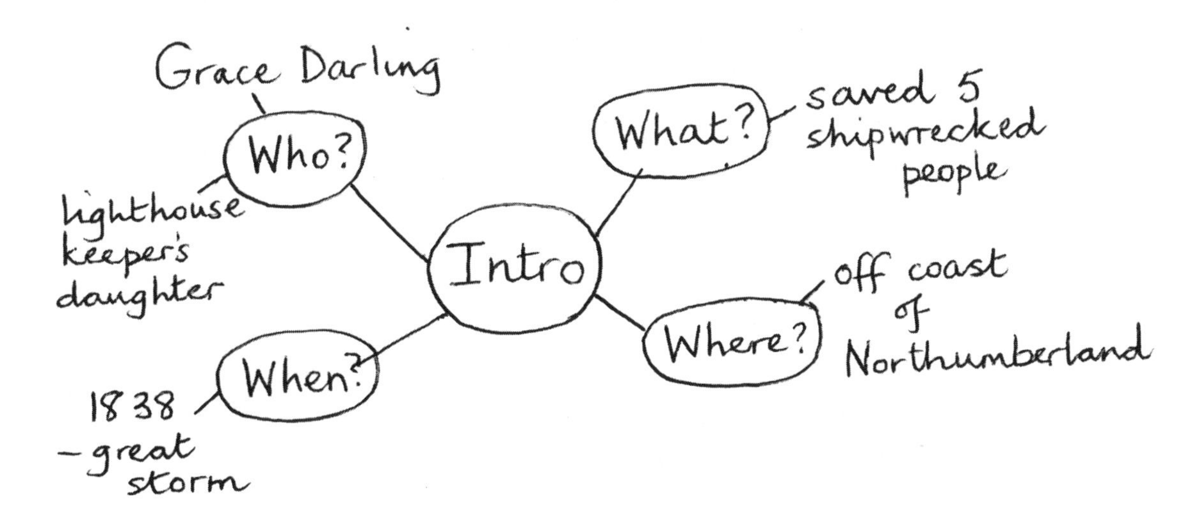

Figure 2.1.3 Introductory paragraph plan

The class discussed how the 'memory-joggers' on the skeleton could be turned into sentences for writing, then used their timelines to write their own versions of the story. Debbie reported that the results were 'amazing':

A supply teacher who knows the class well said:

> *I can't believe the standard of the writing. I think it's because they had the timeline there in front of them, so they didn't have to worry about what to write, they could just concentrate on how to write it. Even the poorer children, who found chronology difficult, just kept referring back to their timelines – I'm sure visual models like this will help develop their memory skills. As for the more able, it freed them up to think about vocabulary and expression – they used some lovely words and phrases, better connectives and more varied sentence openings. The standard improved for every child.*

More ideas

The following list has been compiled from ideas from teachers all over the country who have used timelines with their classes:

- A timeline skeleton does not have to be carefully designed and neatly made. A quick timeline can be created on the whiteboard to remind children of any sequence of events being discussed. This helps reinforce the idea of chronology.
- It isn't important (especially with younger children) to be particularly exact about spacing on the timeline to show the passage of time – a small space for a short time and a larger space for a longer time is quite adequate. However, by Year 2, if you are recording, say, the events of a particular week, or a child's life story, it may be helpful to divide the timeline into roughly equal sections to illustrate days or years.

Figure 2.1.4 Reception children at Sacred Heart Catholic Primary School, Southend-on-Sea using photographs to make a timeline of their day at school

- To ensure children grasp the concept of chronology, timelines should go in a continuous line from left to right. For class timelines you therefore need a long strip of paper – old wallpaper or decorator's lining paper is good, or many educational suppliers do rolls of newsprint or frieze paper.
- Children's pictures or notes can be stuck along the timeline with Blu-tack, or children can write or draw on sticky notes – most stationers now stock lots of shapes, colours and sizes.
- Velcro strip attached along a wall (or even along the top of a storage unit) can be used for any sequencing activity. Pictures or notes on pieces of card with velcro dots can then be stuck along it – children love Velcro!
- Children can hold their pictures or notes and stand in order to create a human timeline. Or cards can be pegged along a washing line.
- For children's own timelines, sugar paper or A3 white paper can be cut into strips (lengthwise) and Sellotaped together. This means they can add more if their timeline grows longer than they expect!
- Other useful materials are fax rolls, adding machine rolls and wallpaper friezes (but the self-adhesive type doesn't work, because you can't write on it). See also speaking and listening activities for Report text, page 3.

Mr Richardson – guide showed us
- saddlestone
- quernstone

sketched mill building

visited millpond – water to drive mill

saw flour bags from old days

Figure 2.1.5 There is great potential for using computers to create skeleton notes, although the shape of the screen means their application with timelines and flowcharts is limited. However, as this example from East Dene School shows, a limited number of pictures displayed across a wide screen (interactive whiteboard) can be very effective

2.2 Report text

Case study 1: healthy and unhealthy foods

Caroline Richardson, at East Dene School in Rotherham, used the spidergram skeleton with her class of five- and six-year-olds as part of their topic work on 'Health'. She used the interactive whiteboard to illustrate how ideas can be organised into categories.

As part of an investigation of healthy and unhealthy food, the children drew pictures of a variety of foods, which were scanned and displayed on the whiteboard. Caroline created two circles, one labelled 'Healthy Foods', and the other 'Unhealthy Foods', and the children then used a pointer to move the pictures so that they were gathered around the appropriate circle.

Caroline then helped the class devise sub-categories – 'fruit' and 'vegetables' for Healthy Foods, and 'sugary foods' and 'fatty foods' for Unhealthy Foods, and created 'arms' on the spidergram for each. The children reorganised the pictures into these sub-categories. They now had a clear visual representation of their discussions about food – a representation of which they had ownership, since it was their own pictures and they had done all the physical manipulation of the images themselves.

Caroline used the whiteboard model as the basis of a variety of writing tasks, depending on children's ability, and noted improvements in the children's writing: 'The pupils have been eager to work in this way and enjoy the visual aspects of the work produced. Using the new technology alongside the skeletons has provided a good working example of the integration of ICT within literacy work, with successful results.'

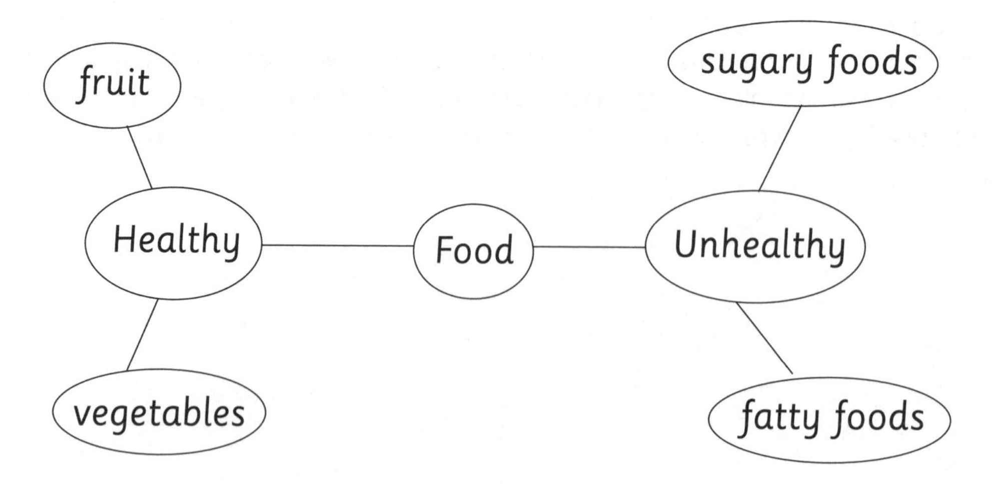

Figure 2.2.1 Spidergram

Case study 2: how we are different

Cecilia Tallon of Sacred Heart Catholic Primary School in Southend-on-Sea developed a large-scale version of the report skeleton to introduce categorisation skills in a Year 2 class (seven-year-olds). As part of their topic work on 'how we are different', the children each came up with one sentence about 'things we like'. These were printed out in large type, so that each child could hold the sentence s/he had composed.

They used a physical sorting activity to group the sentences in hoops laid out on the floor. To start with children stood in the hoop they thought most appropriate, but could move to another if, after discussion, they changed their minds. When this got too busy, they changed to placing the sentence strips in the hoops instead. Categories began to emerge, which they gave broad titles like 'Food', 'Clothes' and 'Hobbies'.

In their literacy lesson, the teacher demonstrated how to write an introductory paragraph, pointing out that people's tastes are different, and summarising the categories to be explored. She then scribed as children from the 'Food' hoop used their sentences to create a paragraph on food preferences. Groups of children, with one acting as a scribe, were then able to write up the facts from the other categories, and their work was gathered together in a class book.

'We also put the hoops on the wall as part of the display,' said Cecilia, 'because the visual impact really helped with the idea of categorisation. I think the opportunity for children to stand in the hoops was useful too – it gave a concrete, physical aspect to an abstract process. The children could see that, if necessary, they could move from hoop to hoop as they organised and reorganised their thoughts.'

Figure 2.2.2 Large-scale activities, like Cecilia Tallon's hoop spidergram, help make the process of organising their ideas more meaningful for children.

Case study 3: seaside holidays

Continuing her topic on the sea (see page 20), Debbie Billard, of East Dene School in Rotherham, used the spidergram report skeleton to help children plan a piece of writing on 'Seaside Holidays'. She used the BOSsing technique described in More ideas (below).

To begin with, the class brainstormed ideas about holidays at the seaside, which Debbie noted on the board. The children then discussed how these ideas could be organised into groups, and chose the headings: 'Things We Do / See / Eat at the Seaside'. Debbie used coloured crayons to indicate the category for each 'memory-jogger', then drew a spidergram diagram and began to fit the information into it.

The more able children understood the principle very quickly and were able to go off and make their own spidergrams, using the brainstorm notes. Debbie suggested turning each arm of the skeleton into coloured seaside buckets, and completed the spidergram on the board with the rest of the class, after which they made their own 'bucket' versions.

The less able children used these notes to write about 'Holidays Now'. In shared work Debbie reminded how to turn each of the 'memory-joggers' on the class spidergram into a sentence and write it. They then continued this process in pairs – making up each sentence orally and then writing it. Debbie found the oral rehearsal particularly successful: 'They even wanted to do their writing as afternoon work – and still got great results!'

Meanwhile, Debbie worked with the more able group to research information about seaside holidays in the past, which created another bucket of memory-joggers. This more able group then used the paired system to write about 'Seaside Holidays, Now and In the Past'. This group could see clearly how the spidergram skeleton organised the information into four separate chunks, so they were able to follow a further instruction when writing up the notes: 'Leave a line after each bucket.' Their writing then fell neatly into paragraphs.

More ideas

The following list has been compiled from ideas from teachers all over the country who have used spidergrams with their classes.

- The steps involved in making a spidergram are summarised in the acronym BOS:
  - **B**RAINSTORM children's knowledge and ideas, noting them in any order.
  - **O**RGANISE the ideas into categories, to create a spidergram. Add more ideas as it develops.
  - **S**PIDERGRAM provides the content for report text with a heading and sub-headings (or just organised into paragraphs).
- During the brainstorming session, children can be asked to jot 'memory-joggers' on to sticky notes. When you are ready to organise their ideas into categories, draw labelled circles and ask them to put their sticky notes in the appropriate place.
- Alternatively, memory-joggers can be written on card and a dab of Blu-tack placed on the back. These can then be moved around in the same way.
- The computer program 'Kidspiration' is designed for 'mapping' spidergrams and other diagrams of this type.
- Children can create human spidergrams by holding a card and standing in a designated area, such as a hoop (as in 'Case study 2' on page 25), which represents their 'category'.

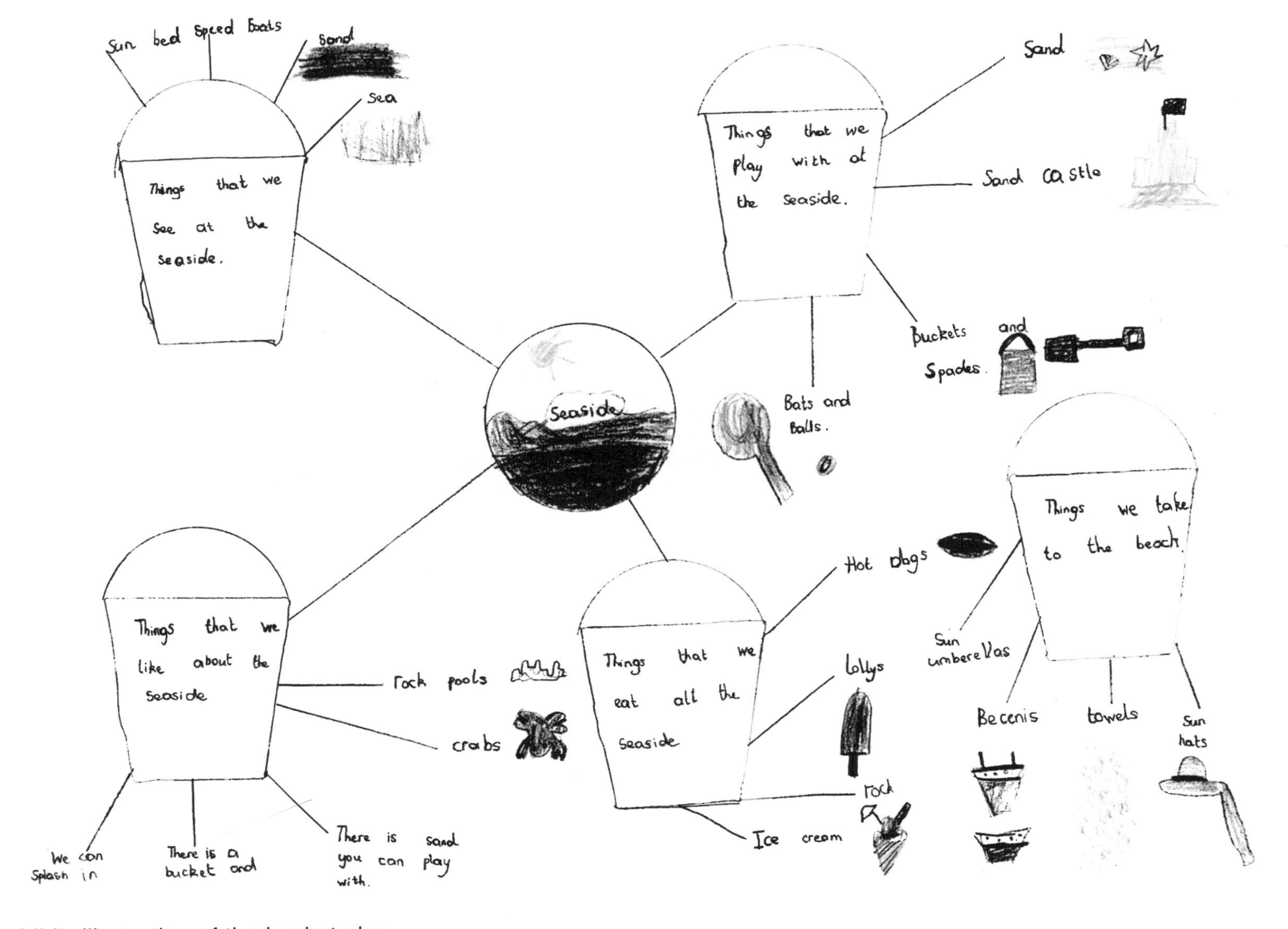

Figure 2.2.3 A child's illustration of the bucket plan

- For a comparative report (e.g. Looking after a pet), it is often helpful to brainstorm and organise information for one type of pet, then use the chosen categories to create a grid, covering several different pets, e.g.:

	dog	cat	gerbil
food			
exercise			
bed			

- For older children, spidergram notes are often much more effective than traditional notes for prepared talks. A simple (and brief) 'memory jogger' acts as a stimulus to the child to talk about what he or she knows, while traditional notes tend to trap the speaker into attempting to follow a sequential pattern which is not easily memorised.

See also speaking and listening activities for Report text, page 3.

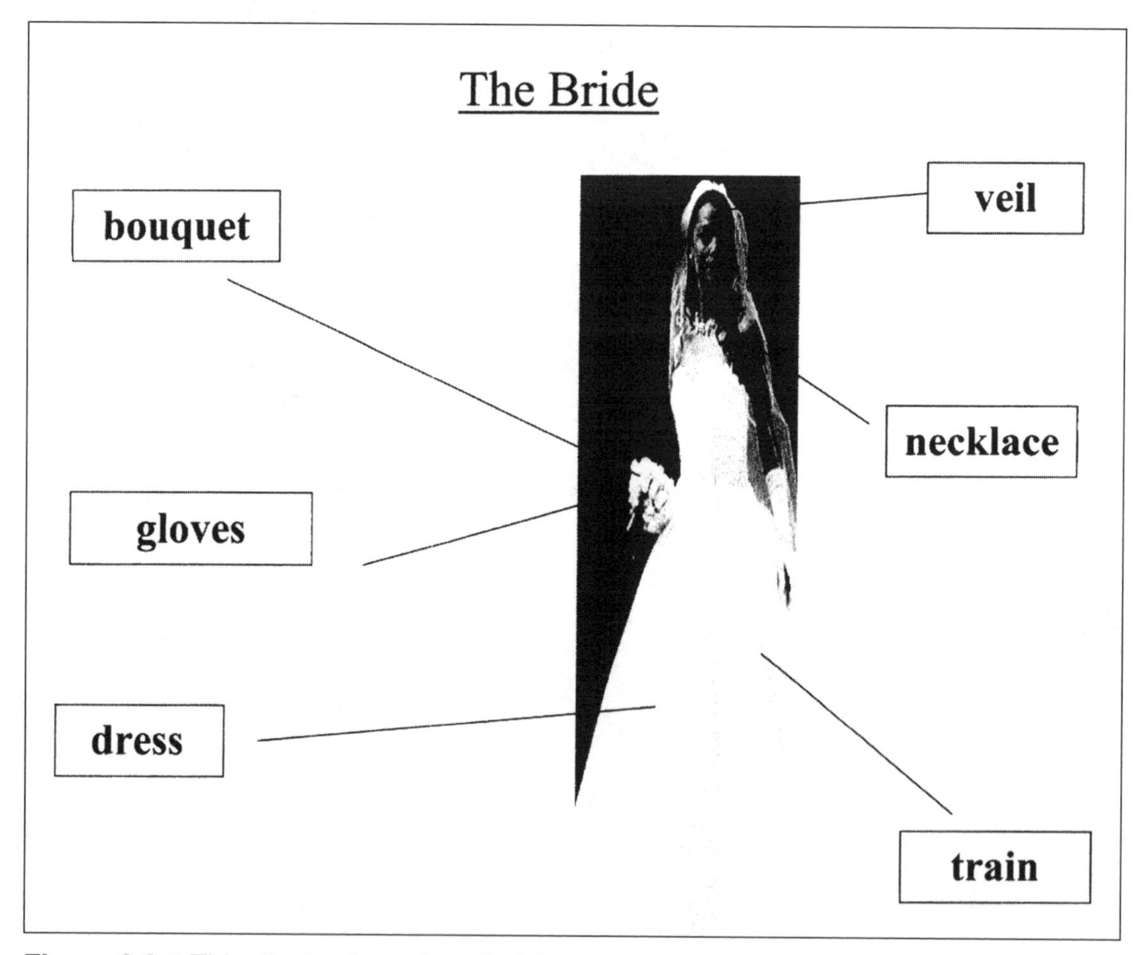

Figure 2.2.4 This display from the 'Wedding' project at Wybourn Primary School, Sheffield, demonstrates how photographs could be used to create spidergram notes

2.3 Instruction writing

Most instructions are a series of sequenced steps, which can be shown on a *flowchart* skeleton. Depending on the age and ability of the children they can use pictures, key words or a mixture of both for this skeleton planning. Making a flow chart helps them sort out the stages in the process and the sequence of events, without the added cognitive burden involved in writing.

Case study 1: honey biscuits

Hayley Williams at Comin Infants School in Aberdare, South Wales, used a flow chart to record the steps in making honey biscuits with her class of seven-year-olds. They had done instructional writing before, so they had plenty of practice of the appropriate language features. She was therefore interested in using a mixture of skeleton planning and focused talk to improve their understanding of the structure of instruction text.

She first modelled how to make a flowchart for making toast, showing the class how to draw the circles and arrows, and how to write notes, not sentences. (They were thrilled to know this was a chance to write without capitals and full stops!) She then demonstrated how to use the finished flowchart to retell the whole process.

Then, after they'd made their honey biscuits, the children made their own flowcharts, with pictures and words for each step. They worked collaboratively, talking through the process, and making decisions about what to include in each step. Hayley reported that this activity was very useful for reinforcing the vocabulary and helping them remember what was involved.

When the children's flowcharts were complete, she revised the layout and language features of instruction text, using this page from *The Key Stage One Skeleton Book* (one of the Skeleton Poster Books).

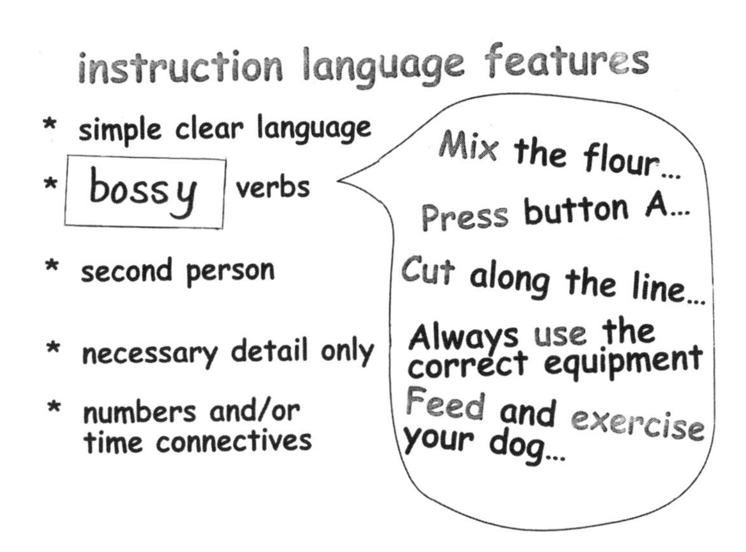

Figure 2.3.1 Instruction language features

She also taught a routine for collaborative writing which would encourage oral rehearsal before they wrote (see page 14), so that they really thought through each sentence.

The children needed a fair amount of time to write up their recipes in this way, but Hayley was convinced that it was worth it:

> *Previously the children had mixed things up or got steps in the wrong order, but with the flowchart to refer to, this didn't happen. They could concentrate on the techniques of writing – putting in the detail, the connectives and so on. It meant they needed very little guidance – the teaching assistant and I moved around chatting to various pairs, but they were able to use their partners to practise sentences. The results were excellent. We couldn't believe how straightforward it was to teach writing in this way. Now we've seen it, it seems so obvious, we can't think why we didn't do it before!*

Case study 2: honey biscuits (four- and five-year-olds)

Mette Cartwright, also in Comin Infants, tried the activity with reception children, using pictures rather than notes. She started by telling them about flowcharts and drew one to show how they work. The next day they made the biscuits, and gathered with Mette to decide how they could draw their flowcharts.She started it off, then the children went off and each did their own. When they had finished, they took it in turns to retell the recipe from the pictures.

Mette reported: 'It was a delight to watch them, and it really focused them on the steps and the sequence! I'll be getting this class next year, and I can already see the next step – accompanying the pictures with a few labels and phrases … it should be a brilliant foundation for when they eventually write the whole recipe.'

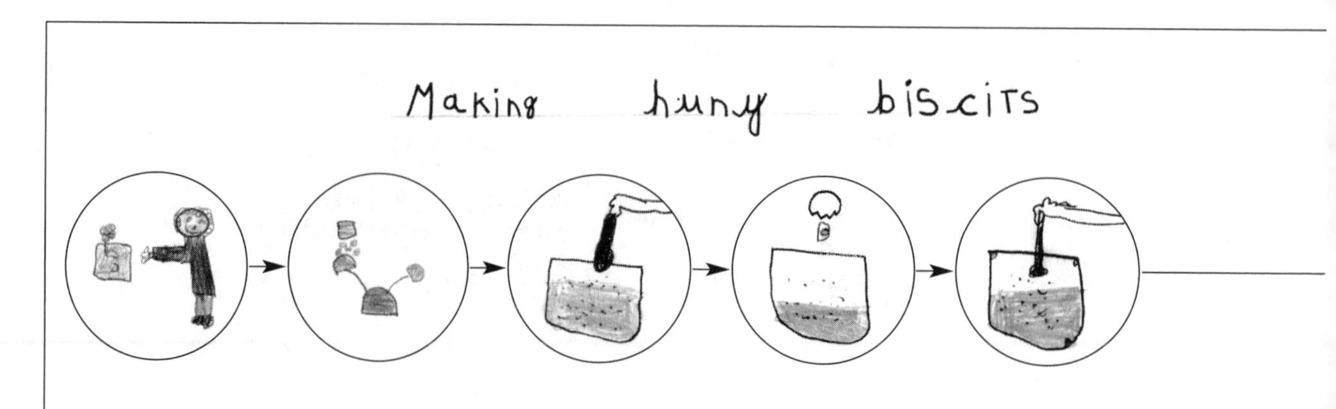

Figure 2.3.2 A recipe flowchart by a five-year-old child from Comin Infants School.

Nasir

HOENY Biscitc.

What you need.

an oven. Cooking fry

Waying scale. Suger.

Flower. Hoeny.

cinnamon. egg.

What you do.

1. Put the oven on at 175°C.
2. Wash yo hands.
3. Way the buter and suger and you must have 120g eche
4. beat the buter and suger until its creme.
5. add a large tablespoon of HonEY.
6. separate The egg York
7. Sture the mixtra togethar.
8. Put a teaspoon of cinnamon.
9. role it until its looks like a.
10. role it until its a bole.
11. Put it in a cooking tryP until 12–15 mins

Then enjoy

Year 2

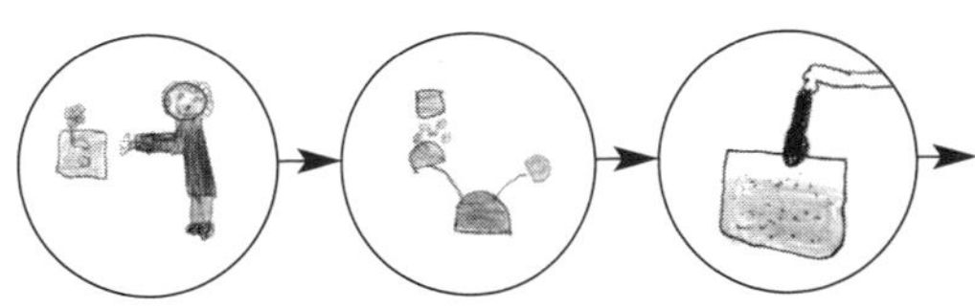

Figure 2.3.3 Above: samples of seven-year-olds' work on instruction writing. Below: the conclusion of the five-year-olds' flowchart.

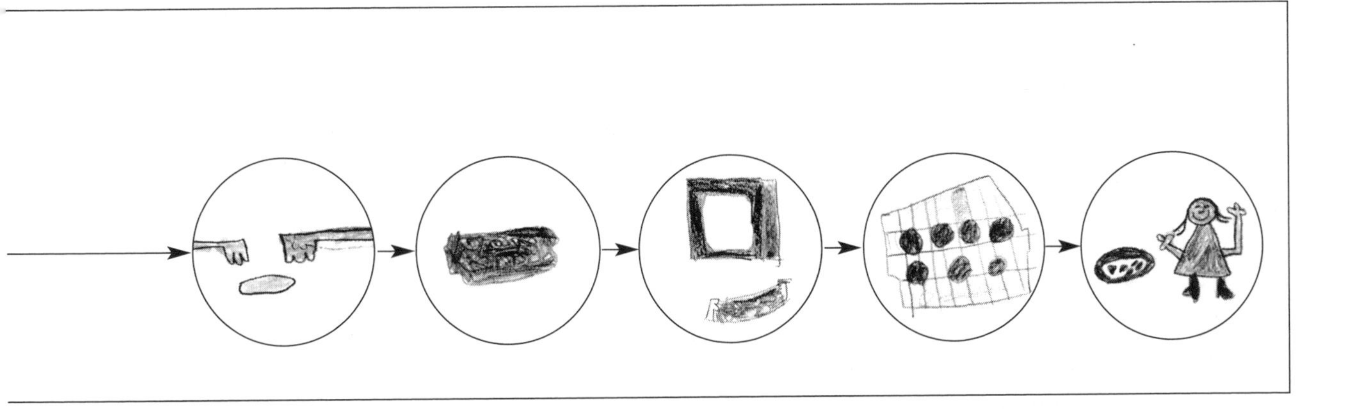

Case study 3: how to cross the road

Kaye Pilcher of Roskear Primary School in Cambourne, Cornwall used an instruction skeleton, along with role play, as part of a school project on safety. Her class of six- and seven-year-olds began with a discussion about road safety in general, and then focused particularly on how to cross a road. Kaye noted the points children made on sticky notes. Many of them related to safe places to cross e.g. 'lollipop lady', 'no parked cars', 'no corners'. Others related to behaviour at the roadside or when crossing the road.

She then modelled how to select and order the sticky notes to make an instruction skeleton for crossing at a zebra, which she wrote up on the board:

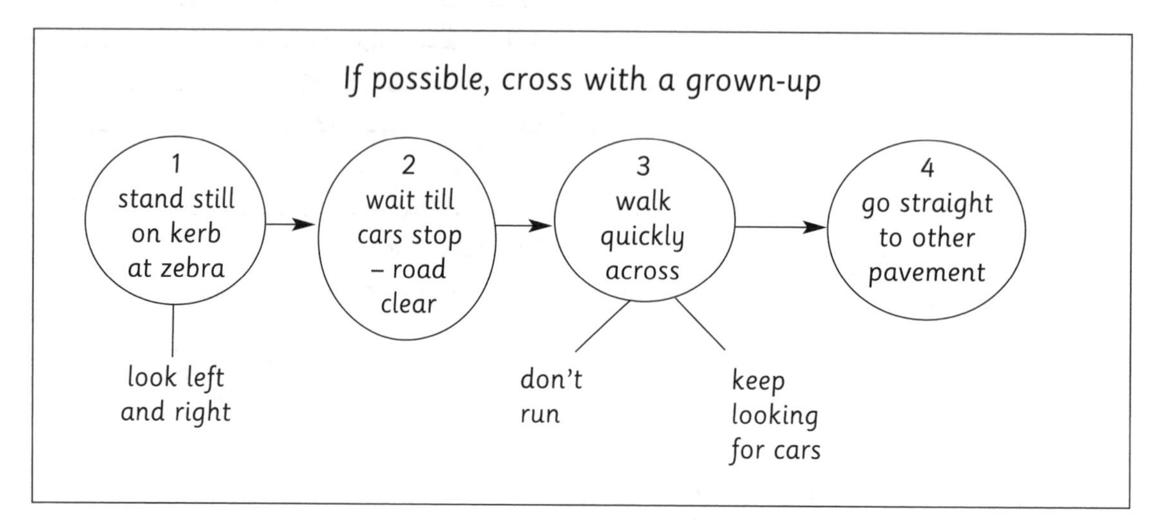

Figure 2.3.4 How to cross the road

Next she asked children in threes to make similar skeleton plans for crossing the road:

- at a pelican crossing;
- at the lollipop lady;
- at a stretch of road with no parked cars or corners.

She worked with a guided group of six on the skeleton for the last scenario, as it was the most difficult.

Next Kaye modelled how to use her zebra skeleton plan as an aide memoire for a role play activity. Two children acted out a road safety 'TV advert', based on the skeleton, while Kaye spoke the instructions. She modelled how to convert the memory-joggers on the 'skeleton script' into spoken sentences (e.g. *This is how to cross the road at a zebra crossing. Step one: stand very still on the kerb at the zebra crossing and look left and right. Step two: wait on the kerb until the cars have stopped and the road is clear.*) Each trio of children then used their own skeleton notes to practise a similar road safety ad, to perform to the class.

Later, the class read and discussed the language and layout of samples of written instruction text. They used a mixture of Shared, Guided and Independent Writing to create their own illustrated information sheet on 'How to cross the road safely'.

More ideas

- There are a number of elements in a piece of instruction writing, not just the sequence of instructions. This page (taken from *The Key Stage One Skeleton Book*) provides a visual prompt:

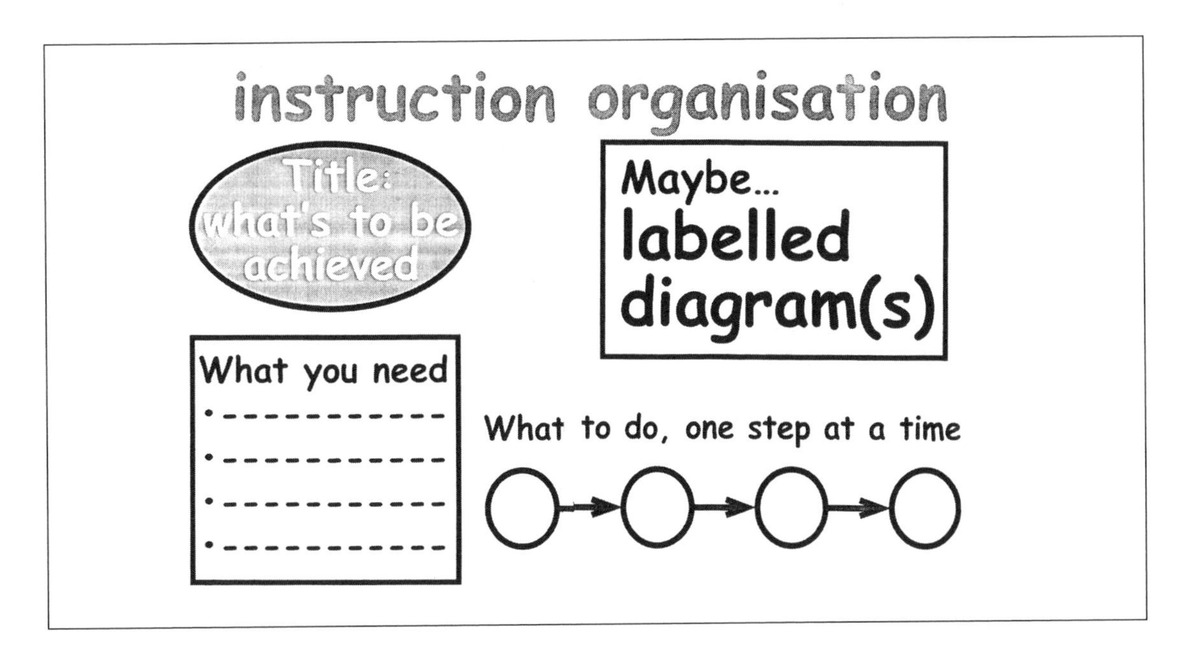

- Instruction skeletons are best drawn from left to right, thus using organisation to indicate time sequence and reinforcing left/right orientation. As for timelines, steps can be drawn horizontally across strips of paper (see page 23), or drawn on card and pegged on a washing line, held by children, or stuck along Velcro strip.
- Sequences of classroom instructions can also be presented in this way – for example, the 'Writing together' poster on page 14.

Figure 2.3.5 Children at Sacred Heart Catholic Primary School in Southend-on-Sea created 'human instructions', using hoops to symbolise the steps in the process. The child in the hoop acted out that step.

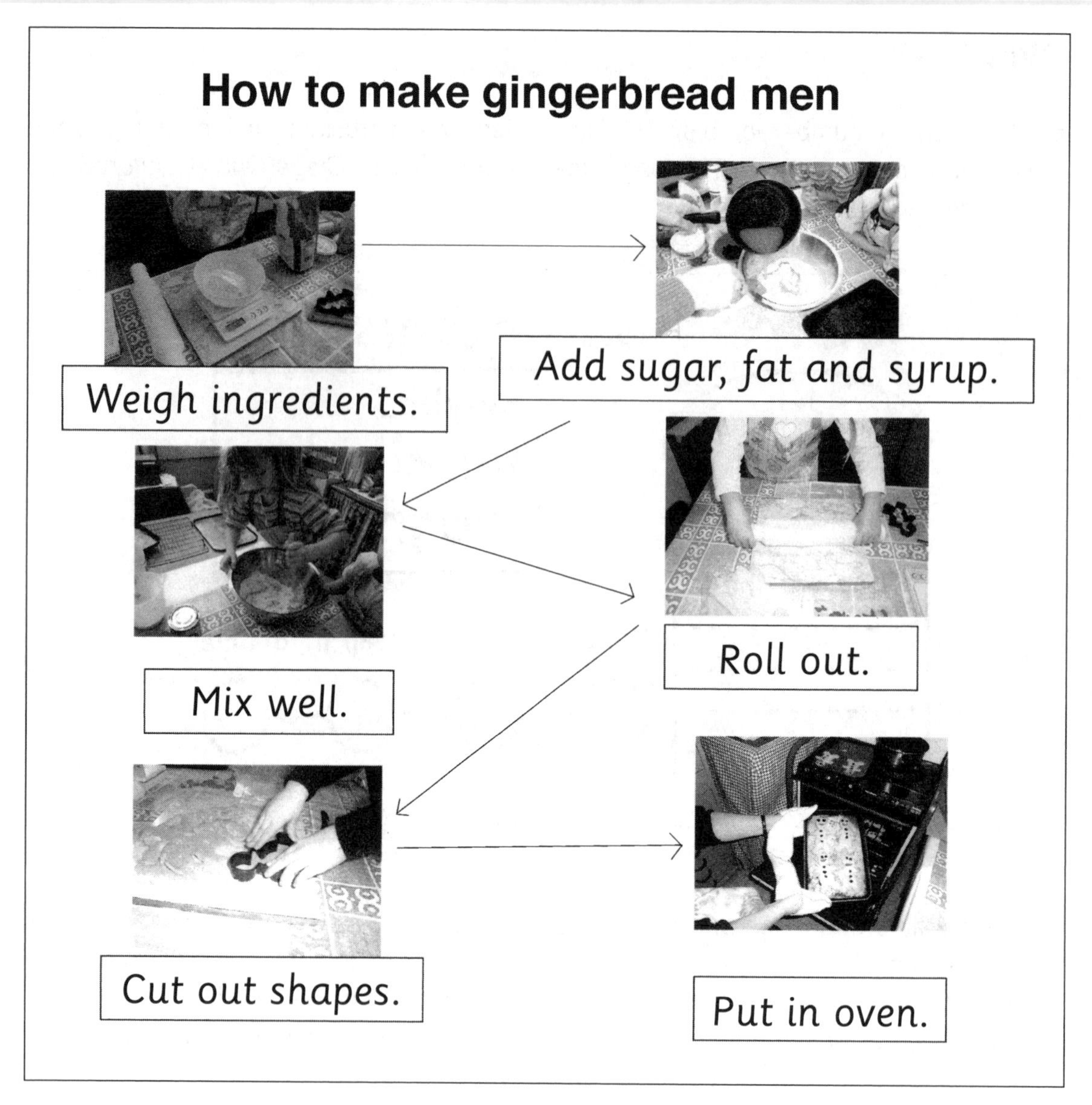

Figure 2.3.6 Illustrations for memory-joggers can be provided by digital camera, as in this example by Debbie Billard of East Dene Primary School, Rotherham. If sequenced instructions for various aspects of classroom practice (e.g. How to switch on the computer) are presented as a flow chart in this way, children will soon be familiarised with the memory-jogging process.

2.4 Explanation writing

Recount, report and instruction writing are common types of non-fiction writing, involving three important underpinning modes of thought: chronology, categorisation and sequenced steps. Explanation writing – requiring an understanding of cause and effect – is much more difficult. The explanation skeleton is, however, similar to that for instructions, since both record processes. Even the under-eights should be able to:

- draw and read flowcharts depicting sequences of cause and effect;
- compose cause-and-effect sentences, using connectives like 'because','so' and 'if'.

Both of these skills can be practised during cross-curricular work on science, geography or history themes.

Case study 1: how babies grow

Rachel Kitchen, Year 2 teacher at Yew Tree Primary School in Dukinfield, Tameside, tried using a flow chart as part of her project on 'Food and Growth'. She began with shared reading of the big book *How Babies Grow* (Longman, 1994), which stimulated a great deal of discussion about babies in the children's own families. Many children had younger siblings and their first-hand knowledge meant they were very interested in the topic.

Rachel produced enlarged copies of the pictures provided in Appendix 3, p. 94, demonstrating child development from birth to two years, and the children helped organise them in order on the board and draw arrows to create a growth flow-chart. They then discussed what they knew about each stage, and drew lines outwards from the pictures to write key words about aspects of development.

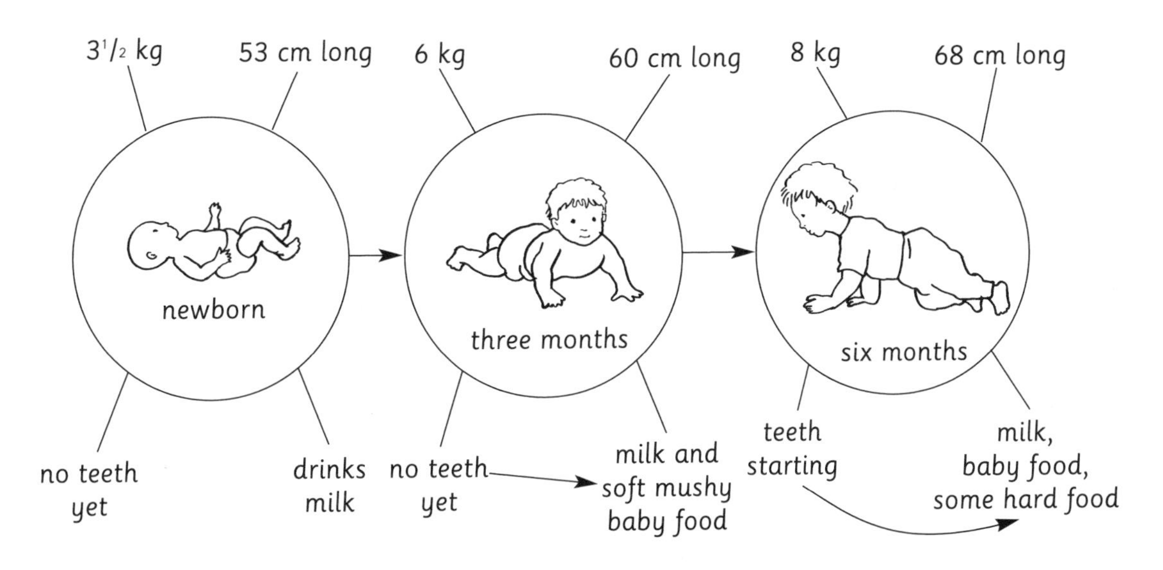

Figure 2.4.1 Baby growth flowchart

Rachel noted that the children had no trouble with the concept of 'key words' in this context: 'When I asked "Why aren't I writing this in sentences?" they gave two reasons: first, there wouldn't be enough room; second, it wouldn't be as easy to read and get the information quickly.'

It led her to question the traditional method of teaching how to take notes:

> *Teachers tend to jump straight into showing how to take notes from books, the way we were taught to do it ourselves – 'We're going to read this page and then we'll identify the key words'. I think that for most children the whole thing must seem pointless and irrelevant, which is probably why they find it so hard. But recording what you've learned on a skeleton is fun and it's meaningful – the 'memory-jogger' words and phrases just come naturally.*

After this demonstration of how to make the flow chart, the pupils tried making them for themselves, using photocopied versions of the same pictures. They worked in pairs, talking through the facts to make their notes. Rachel noted that 'they loved the activity and I felt they had learned a lot more from it than just reading and discussing information from a book.'

The following day they revisited the class flowchart and used it to explore the language of cause and effect. She asked the children to create some sentences about the baby that would answer the question 'Why?' After making up lots of 'why' questions, the children composed sentences to answer them. They did this orally, and used a variety of connectives, for instance:

> 'The baby can eat solid food now **because** it has got teeth.'
> 'The baby has grown stronger now **so** it can stand up.'
> '**When** the baby drinks milk it grows bigger **and** its teeth start to grow.'

Rachel used some of these ideas in a piece of Shared Writing, converting the flowchart notes into the class's own passage about how babies grow. The children helped turn each of the key facts on the flowchart into a sentence, and the layout of the flowchart meant the facts organised themselves naturally into paragraphs.

Rachel felt that skeletons were an aid to good teaching: 'I really like the idea of using diagrams like this as an aid to writing. They help single out the different elements involved in teaching something. You can concentrate first on children's understanding, then on organising and recording the key facts, then on turning what they've learned into sentences.'

Case study 2: ourselves

Peter Scott of Totley Primary School in Sheffield used explanation skeletons as part of a topic on 'Health and Growth'. He introduced children to various types of explanation, starting with the straightforward cause-and-effect model. After an experiment to find out how high pupils could jump, the class created graphs of their efforts which tended to follow this pattern:

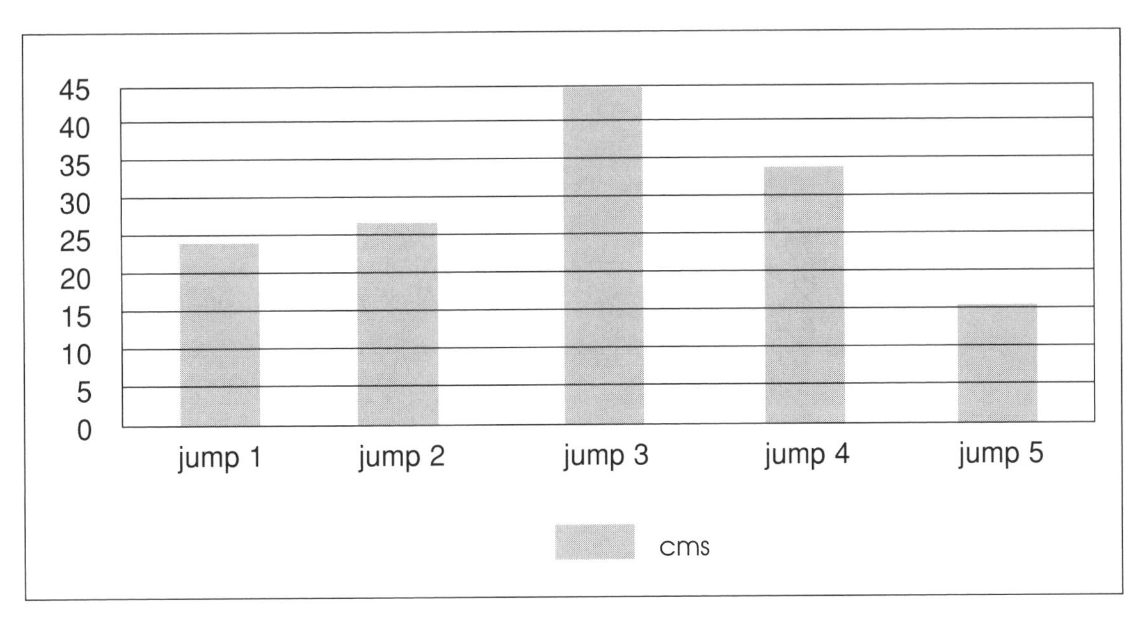

Figure 2.4.2 A graph to show how high Ben can jump

They then discussed the possible reasons for the pattern, and represented them as a linear cause-and-effect flowchart:

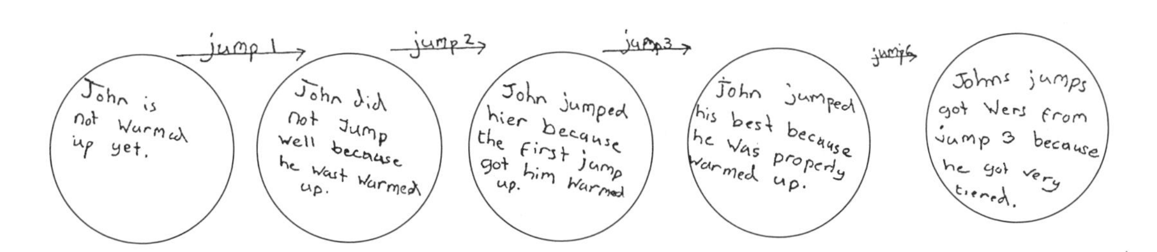

Figure 2.4.3 Linear cause-and-effect flowchart

A general discussion on aspects of healthy living resulted in this multiple-cause flow-chart:

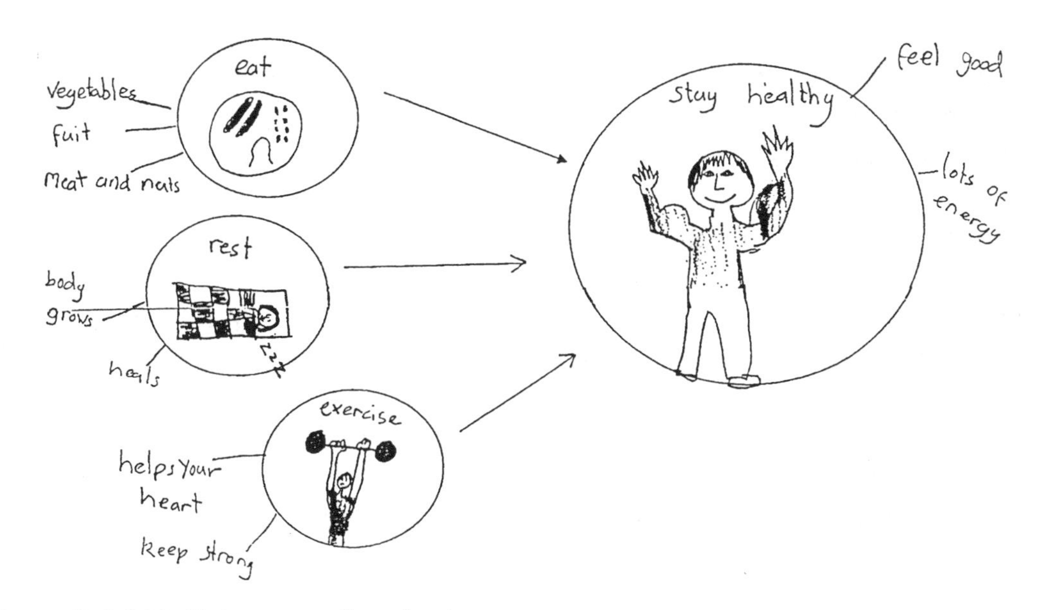

Figure 2.4.4 Multiple-cause flowchart

Discussion about the effects of exercise and rest on the human body produced cycle flowcharts:

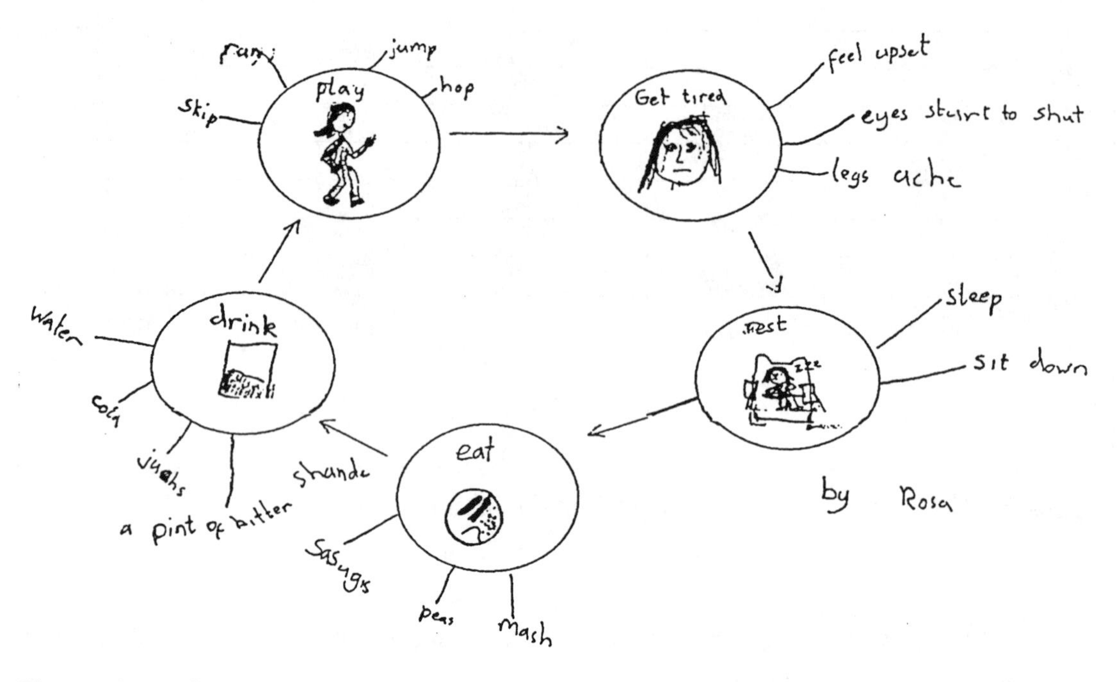

Figure 2.4.5 Cycle flowchart

None of these flowcharts were used as a starting point for writing. Not only is explanation writing extremely difficult (especially for young children), it is often far less effective than a well-drawn diagram. Peter was using skeleton frameworks to familiarise pupils with common structures which underlie many cross-curricular topics – but particularly scientific ideas.

More ideas

The following list has been compiled from ideas from teachers all over the country who have used explanation flowcharts with their classes:

- An explanation skeleton does not have to be carefully designed and neatly made. A quick skeleton can be created on the board to accompany any explanation, and remind children of the key elements and 'make your thinking visible'. Frequent opportunities to view such diagrams will help children see how arrows can be used to indicate cause and effect, and spacial organisation to show the connections between events/ideas.
- Nor is it necessary to get your skeleton notes right first time. Children need to know that it is not easy to represent causal relationships – many are extremely complex, and it takes time to work out a clear visual explanation.
- Incorrect flowcharts are often as useful as successful ones. Peter Scott used this skeleton, purportedly showing 'reversible change', to discuss whether the car's cleanliness and shininess were irrelevant to whether it was moving or stationary.

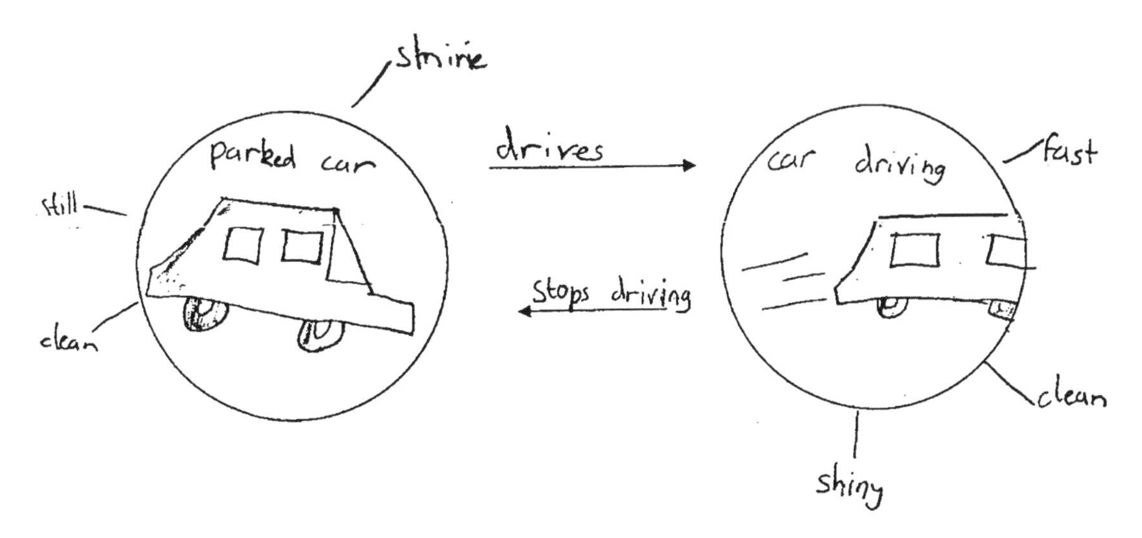

Figure 2.4.6 Reversible change flowchart

PART 3

Teaching materials

3.1 Recount text

Purpose: to retell events in time order – 'a true story'

Text structure

- orientation: setting the scene — who, what, where, when?;
- sequential organisation – what happened, in time order;
- closing statement(s) – bringing the writing to a satisfactory conclusion;
- basic skeleton framework – a **timeline** ('this happened, then this happened', etc.).

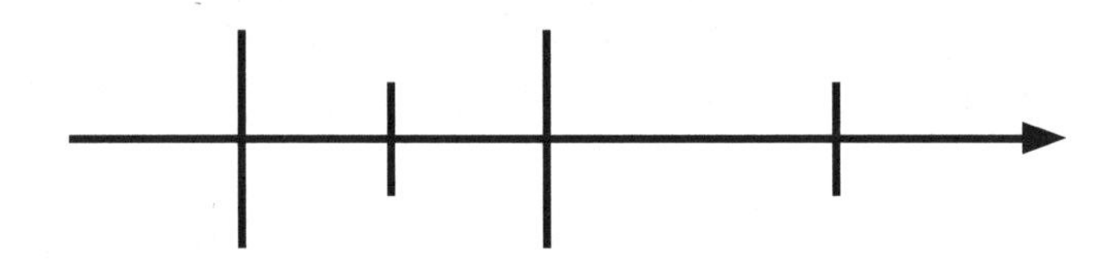

Language features

- past tense (specific events that only happened once);
- time connectives and other devices to aid chronological structure;
- first or third person writing;
- focus on specific participants (this often means proper nouns).

> Don't introduce more than one of these structural or language features at a time.
> Build up children's understanding of the text type gradually.

Key teaching points

Recount is the most common type of non-fiction writing and includes regular 'news' or diary writing; accounts of outings and holiday activities; 'true stories' of events in history or R.E.; and accurate reporting of classroom activities in science or other curriculum areas.

- Young children often need considerable help in organising information into **chronological order**. They often omit or confuse events, especially if facts or experiences are new to them. Preliminary organisation of the content as notes or pictures on a timeline can help children recognise which events are significant and see them as a visual sequence.
- Refer to your notes/pictures as 'memory-joggers', which will help the children when they come to write. You can then ask them to 'Turn each memory-jogger into a sentence'.
- Sometimes, it may not be necessary to turn the memory-joggers into sentences – the timeline may be all that's needed to record understanding.
- With older children, the completed timeline may also be used as a paragraph planner. Before they start to write ask them to draw red lines through the timeline to show where there is a natural break in the story. You can then suggest: 'When you come to a red line, miss a line in your book and start a new sentence.'

> Common forms of **recount text**:
>
> - letter;
> - biography or autobiography;
> - diary or journey;
> - newspaper or magazine report;
> - non-fiction book (e.g. history);
> - encyclopaedia entry;
> - write-up of a trip or activity;
> - account of science experiment.

MY LIFE SO FAR

My name is Jessica Martin and I am six years old. I live in York with my mum and my little brother Baz. This is the story of my life so far.

I was born at St Mary's Hospital on 19th December, 2004. I was a good baby and did not keep Mum awake much at night. When I was 3, Baz was born. He was not a good baby! He cried all the time and kept us all awake.

Not long after Baz was born, I started at nursery and met my best friend Hannah. We had lots of fun playing in the house and dressing up. At the age of 4, I had chicken pox. It made me very itchy and Mum dabbed my spots with pink medicine.

Soon after that, I started school. Hannah and I were in Mrs Robinson's class. It was fun because we played all day. Next we went into Mrs Bennett's class. That was when I learned to read and write. Mrs Bennett read us lots of stories.

Last September I moved up into Mr Long's class, and now I am learning my times tables.

Shared reading of 'My life so far'

The passage can be used for one or more of the following, depending on children's age and ability.

Introducing timelines

Read a passage to the children then demonstrate how to turn the text into time line:

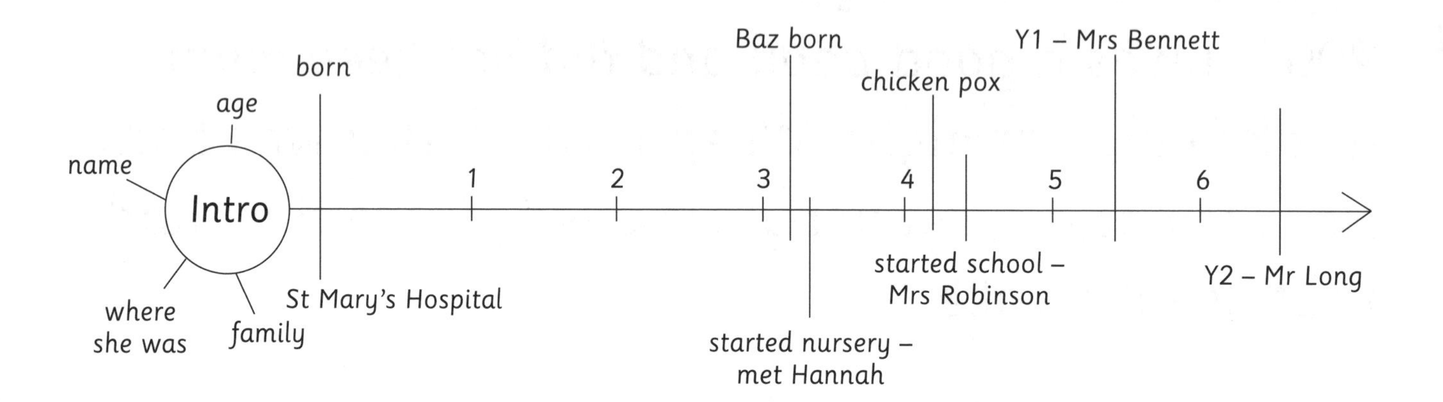

An introductory paragraph

Reread the introductory paragraph.

This is report text, telling the reader some essential facts about the author before the life story begins. Establish that it covers name, age, where she lives, who is in her family. Use as a speaking frame for planning introductory paragraphs about the children themselves (see page 12):

My name is __________ *and I am* __________ *years old. I live in* __________ *with* __________ *This is the story of my life.*

Ask children to express the same information about themselves in other ways, always using sentences.

The language of time

Reread from the beginning of paragraph 2, where the piece becomes recount text.

Ask the children to look for ways in which the author shows time passing (highlighted) and collect on a poster:

- giving dates;
- sentence openings like *When I was three* ... and *At the age of four* ...;
- simple time connectives: *next, now.*

Note that author never uses *then* and never uses the same expression twice.

Discuss how these 'signposts' help the reader keep track of the life story and show you that it is being written in time order.

Over time, add further time connectives (and other devices for showing the passage of time) to your poster, collected from other recount texts.

[Older/more able pupils: Ask pupils to reread passage, a paragraph each. Mark paragraph breaks on the timeline, and note how paragraphs reflect the most significant events in Jessica's life.]

Keeping the reader's interest

Help children notice how Jessica structures her retelling – for each separate event, she states the fact, and then gives at least one interesting detail, e.g.:

- facts of her birth – she was a 'good baby';

- Baz's birth – not a good baby!;
- joined nursery – fun with Hannah;
- chicken pox – pink medicine.

Older children could follow this structure in their own writing.

Capital letters for proper nouns

Ask pupils to re-read the passage, a sentence each. Mark capital letters at the beginning of sentences. Discuss why other words have capital letters. Collect examples of names of people, places, months and forms of address (Mr, Mrs). Note also the use of capitals to make the title stand out.

Note (children do not need to know this, but just in case someone asks!) The word Mum is sometimes used as a proper noun (in which case it needs a capital), and sometimes as a common noun (as in paragraph one: 'my mum', like 'my brother').

Ask pupils to state/write some proper nouns associated with themselves, which need capital letters.

Continue your collection of capital letters for proper nouns from your reading of other texts.

Investigating tense

Ask pupils to reread the first two paragraphs. Can they spot that one is about 'now' and one is about

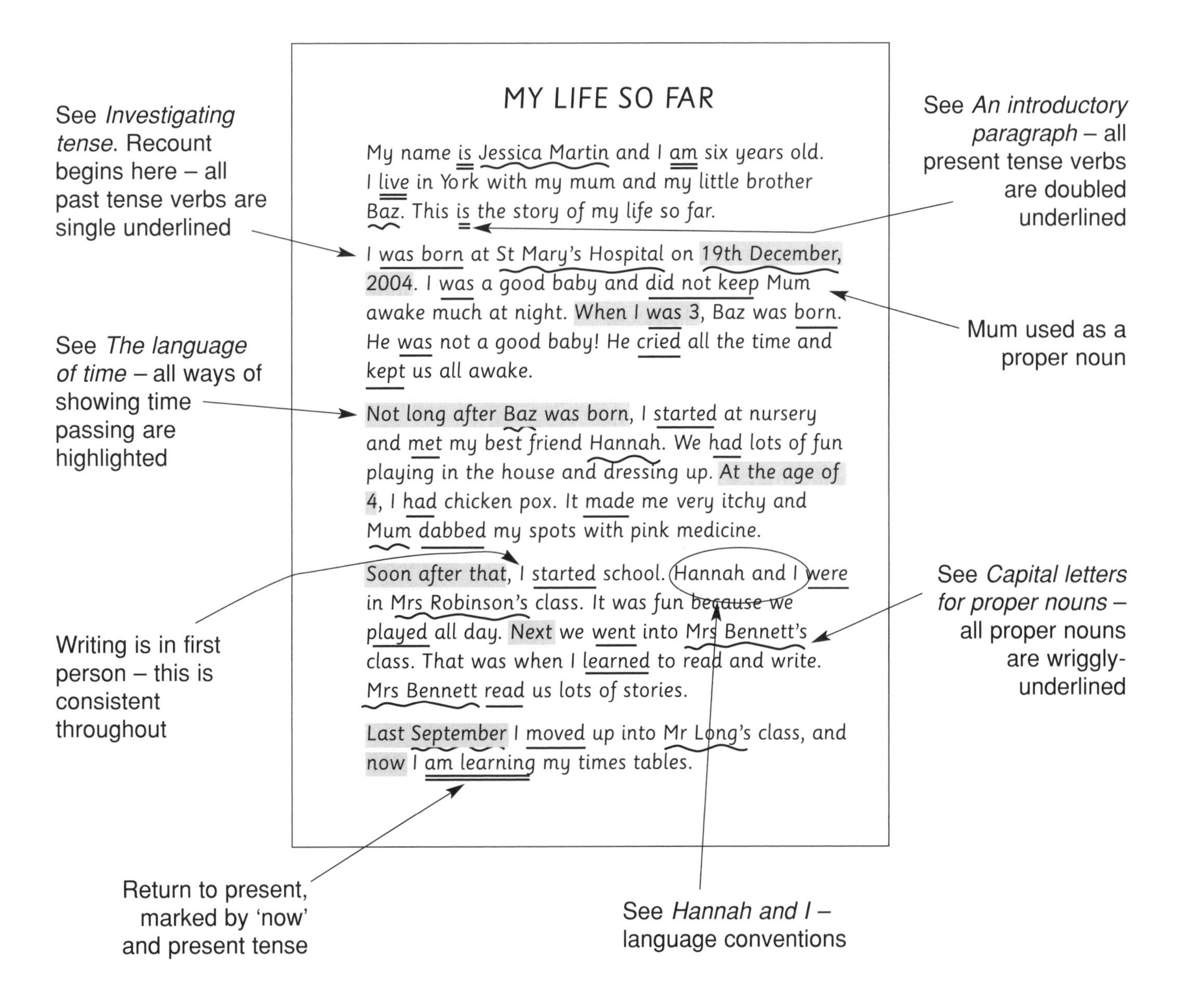

'the past'? How do they know where the change happens? Guide them to a recognition of the change of tense between *I live* and *I was born.* Many of the verbs in the passage feature the -ed ending (there are examples of all spelling rules associated with it: cry – cried; dab – dabbed; move – moved). Others are common irregular past tenses, and there are two examples of verb chains (*was born* and *did not keep*).

Regular past tense			*Irregular past tense*			
cr**i**ed	da**bb**ed	learned	was	met	made	went
started	played	mov**ed**	kept	had	were	read

Hannah and I

In the penultimate paragraph, Jessica refers to Hannah and I. Explain that this is the conventional order when writing about yourself and another person (or persons). As well as being grammatical, it is also polite because you are putting the other person first.

Ask pupils to work in pairs to think of two things they and their partner both like doing. They should then report back to the group using these speaking frames:

Partner 1: ________ and I both like ________.
Partner 2: _________ and I also enjoy _______.

Shared Writing of 'My life so far'

Lesson 1: collecting ideas and making a timeline

Talk about children's own life stories and significant events. Collect ideas for the sorts of things they might write about. Decide roughly how many events you want them to write about (each event should take one writing lesson).

Give each child a timeline frame (see page 47) and help them write their name, age, place they live and family (those with huge families could write, e.g. *my mum, dad, 5 sisters and 3 brothers).* Depending on the age/ability of pupils, you could provide this information for them, ask them to work it out and check their answers through a 'show me' activity on individual whiteboards, or expect them to fill in the details independently.

Demonstrate how to fill in the timeline for yourself (up to the age of six or seven).

Ask the children to take their timelines home to choose details to write about. Parents may also wish to send in photographs to help illustrate the finished piece of writing.

Lesson 2: writing an introductory paragraph

Remind children of the 'speaking frame' used earlier. Depending on the age/ability of the children, you may choose to use this for Shared Writing, or devise another way of presenting the information.

Write an introductory paragraph for yourself (aged six). Demonstrate how to write the first sentence. Ask pupils to compose the second sentence and scribe for them. Ask pupils in pairs to compose and write a third sentence like the original 'This is the story of my life so far'. Choose one and scribe it. During Shared Writing remind children as appropriate about sentence level features covered earlier, e.g. capital letters.

Children should now write the title and introductory paragraph on their own life story.

Lesson 3: telling the story

Remind children how each time you write a fact you write a sentence or so of detail about it.

Provide a 'speaking frame' for the first sentence: 'e.g. I was born at _______ on _______.' Ask pupils to fill it in (see page 47). Model how to write your first paragraph – fact detail; fact detail. Use:

- demonstration writing for the first sentence;
- scribing for the sentence of detail;
- supported composition for the 'way of showing time passing' leading into the next fact.

During Shared Writing remind children as appropriate about sentence level features covered earlier, e.g. **past tense.**

Lessons 4 and 5: continue in the same way to continue the life story

My life so far

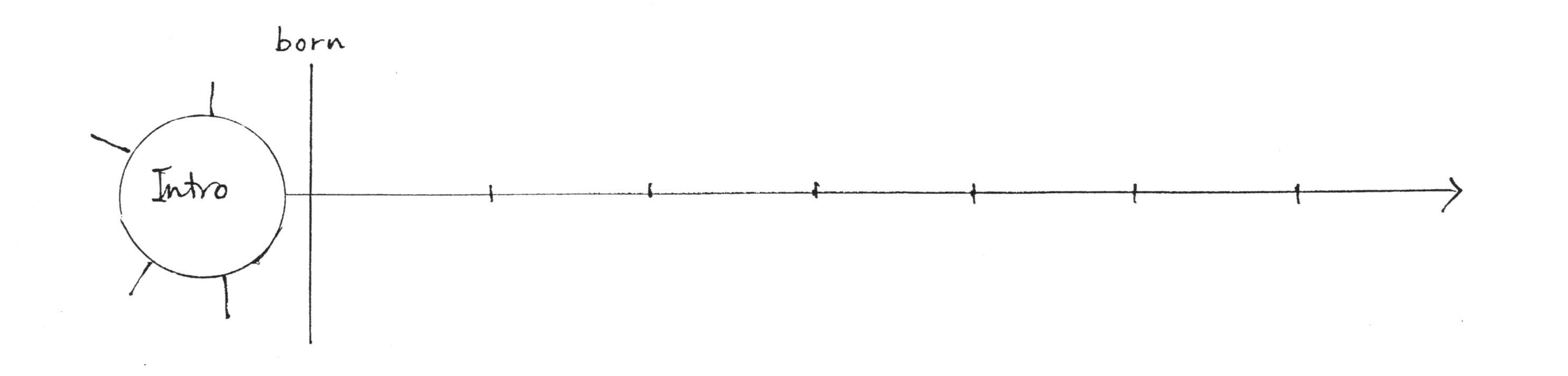

We are going to write our life stories. First we are going to plan them on a timeline (like the example below). Please will you help your child think of .... important events in .... life so far, and put 'memory joggers' on the timeline. Memory joggers can be words, phrases or even little pictures, as long as your child can remember what they stand for. Please talk about each event with your child and make sure .... knows some detail about it.

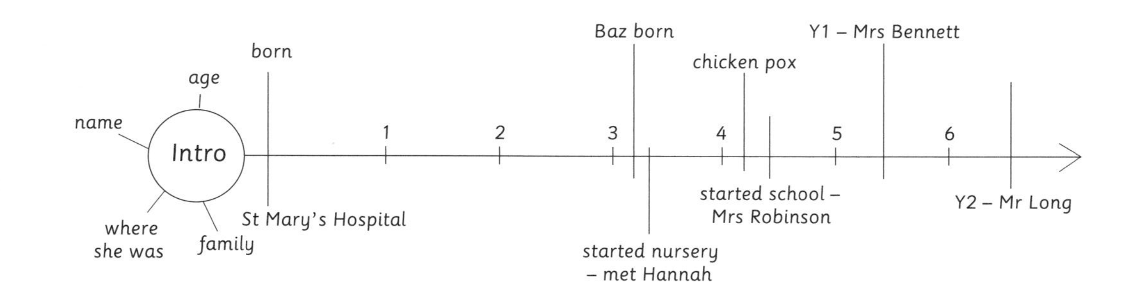

3.2 Report text

Purpose: to describe the characteristics of something

Text structure

- introductory information about what is to be described: who, what when, where (overall classification);
- non-chronological organisation;
- description organised according to categories of information;
- basic skeleton framework – a **spidergram** (one spider leg per category, which could divide into further spider legs, depending on degree of detail.

Language features

- present tense (except historical reports);
- usually general nouns and pronouns (not particular people or things);
- third person writing;
- factual writing, often involving technical words and phrases.

Don't introduce more than one of these structural or language features at a time.
Build up children's understanding of the text type gradually.

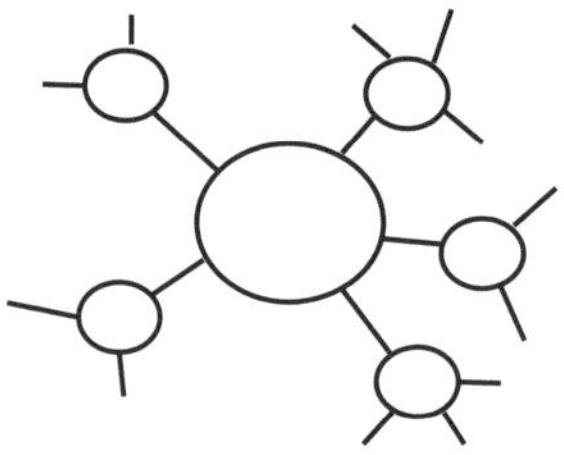

Key teaching points

- The difference between report and recount is that report text is usually non-chronological (although there are occasional reports which may be chronologically organised, e.g. a generalised *Day in the Life of ...* which is not about a specific day or person). The basic skeletons for the two text types show this difference clearly.
- Learning to organise report text involves learning to categorise information. There are three stages in making a spidergram (which we have called BOSsing – described on page 26), and many children find the process challenging. It is, however, worth the effort to teach it well, as categorisation is an important thinking skill.
- There are other ways of representing report text (e.g. a picture, labelled diagram, plan or map) which may be used instead of or in addition to the spidergram. Many reports are comparative, in which case a grid may be the most appropriate skeleton.

Common forms of **report text**:

- information leaflet;
- school project file;
- tourist guide book;
- encyclopaedia entry;
- magazine article;
- non-fiction book (e.g. geography);
- letter.

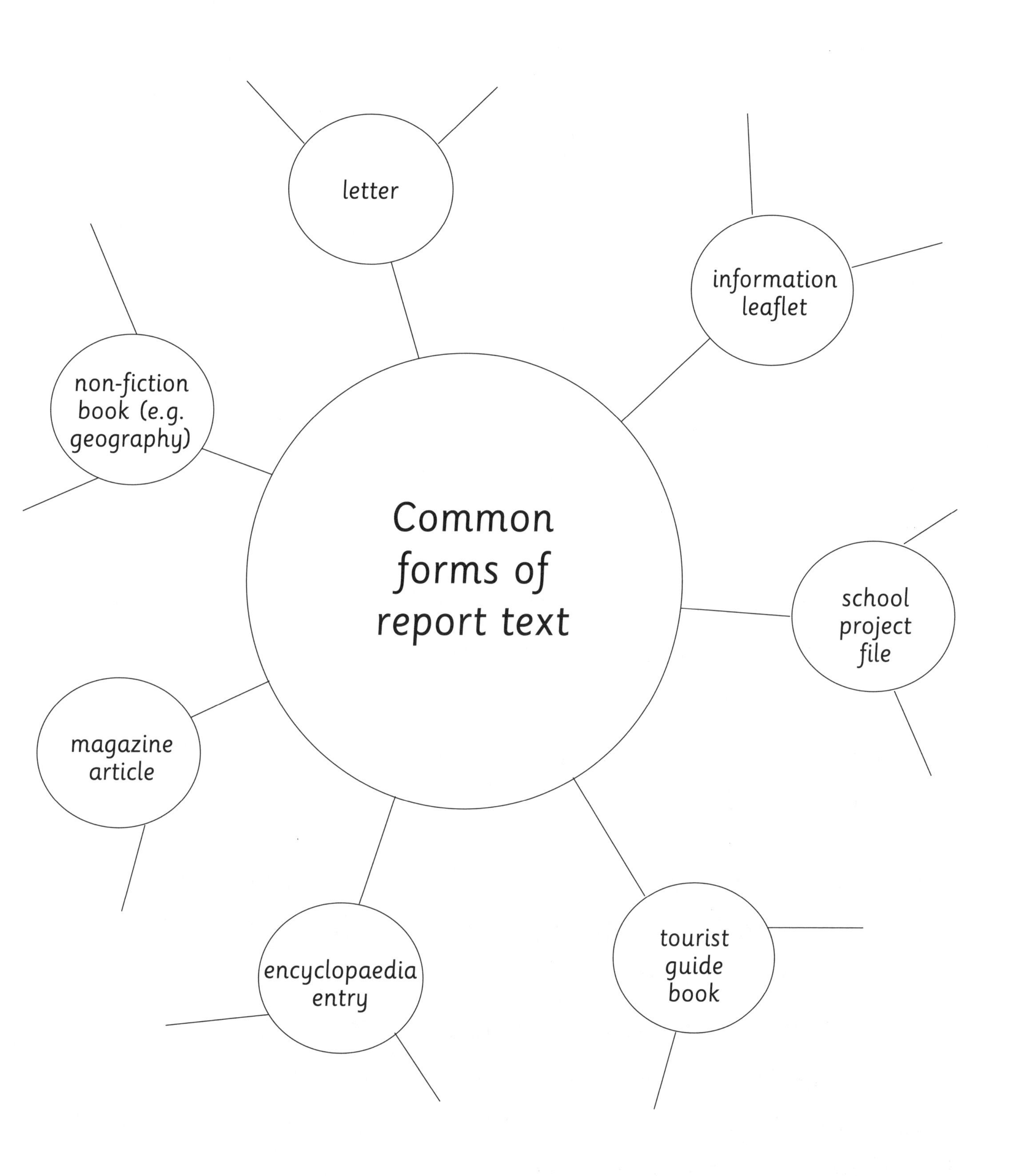
Common forms of report text
letter
information leaflet
non-fiction book (e.g. geography)
school project file
magazine article
encyclopaedia entry
tourist guide book

OUR SCHOOL

Our school is called Lee Park Primary, and it is in Longton near York. Lee Park has seven classes, from Reception to Year 6, and there are 198 pupils in the school. It was built in 1965.

Lee Park has a big playground, with special sections for the infants and the juniors. In the infant playground there are lots of shapes painted on the ground, like hopscotch squares and a map of Britain, for people to play on. There is also a special area for sitting quietly. The junior playground has play areas marked out as well, including football and netball pitches.

We also have a school field. This is next to the school down a little lane. In the summer we are allowed to play on the field too, but in winter it is too muddy. However, when it snows, Mrs Carr (our headteacher) sometimes lets us go on the field.

The school has a big school hall that we use for assembly and for some lessons, such as gym and drama. We also use the hall for lunches. You can bring packed lunch and sit at the back of the hall, or you can have a school lunch. The dinner ladies serve this on long wooden tables at the front of the hall. The rest of the time, the tables are stored in a cupboard.

Shared reading of 'Our school'

The passage can be used for one or more of the following, depending on children's age and ability.

Making spidergrams

Read passage to children then demonstrate how to turn the text into a spidergram. Help the children to see that each paragraph (an arm of the spider-gram) is about a particular topic.

Discuss how putting all the facts about a certain topic together helps the reader keep track of the details. Since descriptions are not written in time order, you need some way of organising all the information.

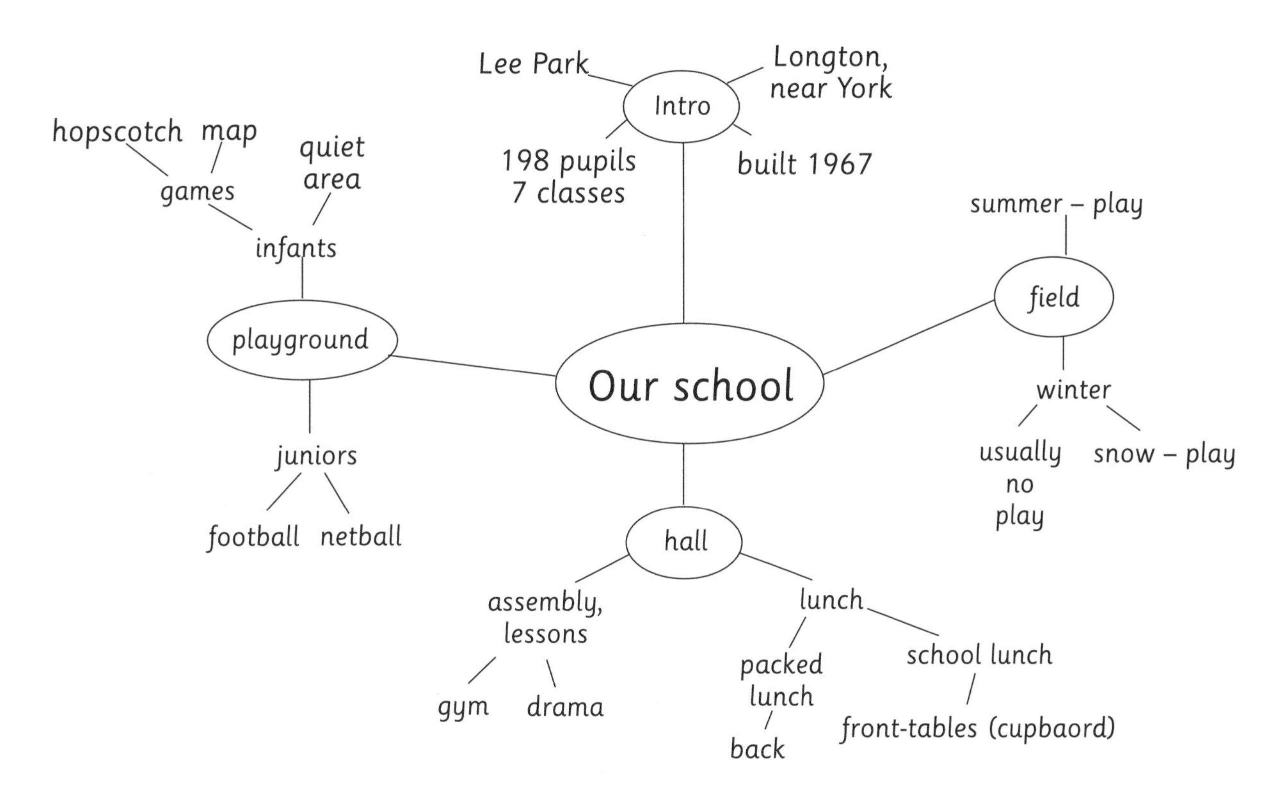

An introductory paragraph

Reread the introductory paragraph.

This is report text, telling the reader some essential facts about the school as a whole. Establish that it covers the name, where it is, number of classes and pupils, date when built. Provide (or discuss/send pupils to research) the same facts for your school, and note these as memory-joggers on the board.

Use the unfinished sentences below as a speaking frame for an introductory paragraph about your school (see page 12):

Our school is called ________, and it is in __________ . ___________ has __________ classes, and there are __________ pupils in the school. It was built in ________ .

Then ask children in pairs to think of other ways of turning the memory-joggers into sentences. In seeking responses, stress a variety of sentence openings.

Sorting out information

Reread from the beginning of paragraph two and, without referring to your spidergram notes, ask children what the main topic of each paragraph is. Note how the first words of each paragraph introduce the topic (see highlighting opposite).

Display the spidergram and show how, from paragraph two, the information in each paragraph is split into two parts – sometimes it's then split up even further. Appoint two children, an 'infant' and a 'junior', to read the first sentence of paragraph two like this:

Both: *Lee Park has a big playground, with special sections for*
Infant reader: *the infants*
Both: *and*
Junior reader: *the juniors.*

Ask pupils in pairs to appoint themselves 'infant' and 'junior' and read paragraph two. 'Infant' should read all the bits about the infant playground, 'junior' should read all the bits about the junior playground. Get one pair to demonstrate, then discuss how the author makes it very clear which playground he is talking about (*In the infant playground ... There is **also** ... The junior playground ...*).

OUR SCHOOL

Our school is called Lee Park Primary, and it is in Longton near York. Lee Park has seven classes, from Reception to Year 6, and there are 198 pupils in the school. It was built in 1965.

Lee Park has a big playground, with special sections for the infants and the juniors. In the infant playground there are lots of shapes painted on the ground, like hopscotch squares and a map of Britain, for people to play on. There is also a special area for sitting quietly. The junior playground has play areas marked out as well, including football and netball pitches.

We also have a school field. This is next to the school down a little lane. In the summer we are allowed to play on the field too, but in winter it is too muddy. However, when it snows, Mrs Carr (our headteacher) sometimes lets us go on the field.

The school has a big school hall that we use for assembly and for some lessons, such as gym and drama. We also use the hall for lunches. You can bring packed lunch and sit at the back of the hall, or you can have a school lunch. The dinner ladies serve this on long wooden tables at the front of the hall. The rest of the time, the tables are stored in a cupboard.

present tense for report writing

one past tense verb referring to history

See *Sorting out information.* All topic sentences are highlighted

See *The word 'and'.* 'and' is underlined throughout. Other words signalling extra information are double-underlined

See *Giving examples.* Words signalling examples have wiggly underlining

capital letters for proper nouns (see activity for Recount, page 44)

The word 'and'

Ask pupils to reread the passage, a sentence each, while the class watches out for the word 'and'. After each sentence, highlight all the 'ands'. Help children note that, in writing, 'and' is always in the **middle** of the sentence, never at the beginning (see page 86 in Appendix 1 on Grammar). Talk about how 'and' is used to link ideas together, but if it is overused, it can become very boring. Using an enlarged copy of page 54, demonstrate the effects of overusing 'and'. By comparing this to our original text, help children see that the author avoids these problems by:

- splitting his ideas up into sentences – no more than two ideas linked by 'and' in any one sentence;
- sometimes using other words to show that he is giving extra information: 'too', 'as well', 'also'.

Help the children recognise that 'and' is an important word and we couldn't do without it, but it should not be overused.

Giving examples

Before rereading the passage, point out that, when the author is describing aspects of the school, he often gives examples to show what he means more clearly. Can pupils spot occasions when he does this? Draw attention to the examples and the words (in bold below) that signal to the reader that we are going to hear some examples.

> '... shapes painted on the ground, **like** hopscotch squares and a map of Britain ...'
> '... play areas marked out, **including** one for football and one for netball...'
> '... some lessons, **such as** gym and drama ...'

Provide the following speaking frames for pupils to fill in (see page 12):

> 'Some of our class have long names, **like** ...'
> 'There are many boys in our class, **including** ...'
> 'Our class does lots of lessons, **such as** ...'

Mention two other useful 'signal phrases' with which writers can start 'example sentences': 'For example ... ', 'For instance ...'

Older or more able children should be able to think of sentences about other topics in which they can use the 'signal words' to introduce examples.

Shared Writing: a class book about 'Our school'

Lesson 1: writing an introductory paragraph

Remind children of the 'speaking frame' used earlier. Depending on the age/ability of the children, you may choose to use this for Shared Writing, or devise another way of presenting all the information it covers.

Explain that you are going to write an introductory paragraph for a class book called 'Our school'. Demonstrate how to write a first sentence. Ask pupils to compose a second sentence and scribe for them. Ask pupils in pairs to compose and write a third sentence. Choose one and scribe it. During Shared Writing remind children as appropriate about sentence level features covered earlier, e.g. capital letters.

Children should now write their own introductory paragraphs. Pick the best of these to use in the class book.

Lesson 2: finding out

Organise for groups to go on 'fact-finding walks' around the school, on which they can talk to each other and their group leader (teacher? classroom assistant? parent helper?) about the building and facilities.

Lesson 3: brainstorming

Ask pupils to think of facts about the school that they think should be included in the book. Get them to jot these in memory-jogger form on individual sticky notes, and stick on a board. Discuss how you will group your ideas for writing, and draw a spidergram frame with labelled categories. Ask children to group the sticky notes around the appropriate categories.

Can children think of more facts to put in each category? – add extra sticky notes.

Where there are a lot of notes in a category, talk about ways you could create subcategories – draw extra spider-legs and regroup the sticky notes.

Lesson 4: turning memory-joggers into sentences

Take one of the spidergram arms, and model how to write it up. Demonstrate how to turn one memory-jogger into a sentence (or you may link two with 'and'). Create more sentences through scribing and supported composition. Emphasise aspects of composition covered in previous teaching.

In Independent Writing, ask:

- less able children to write up the paragraph you have just demonstrated;
- other children to write up other paragraphs in the same way.

Choose the best to make a class book about 'Our school' and ask pupils to illustrate it.

OUR SCHOOL

('and' version)

Our school is called Lee Park Primary, and it is in Longton near York and it has seven classes, from Reception to Year 6, and there are 198 pupils in the school and it was built in 1965.

Lee Park has a big playground, with special sections for the infants and the juniors and in the infant playground there are lots of shapes painted on the ground, like hopscotch squares and a map of Britain, for people to play on and there is a special area for sitting quietly and the junior playground has play areas marked out, including football and netball pitches.

And we have a school field and this is next to the school down a little lane and in the summer we are allowed to play on the field too, but in winter it is too muddy. However, when it snows, Mrs Carr (our headteacher) sometimes lets us go on the field.

The school has a big school hall that we use for assembly and for some lessons, such as gym and drama and we use the hall for lunches and you can bring packed lunch and sit at the back of the hall, or you can have a school lunch and the dinner ladies serve this on long wooden tables at the front of the hall and the rest of the time, the tables are stored in a cupboard.

3.3 Instruction text

Purpose: to tell someone how to do or make something.

Text structure

- title or opening sets out **what's to be achieved**;
- starts with **list** of items required;
- often accompanied by **diagram**(s);
- sequenced steps in to achieve the goal – what to do, **in time order;**
- skeleton framework – a **flowchart** ('you do this then you do this, etc.').

Language features

- **'bossy** verbs' (technical name: imperative);
- in time order (often **numbered** steps and/or **time connectives**);
- all necessary **detail** included (e.g. quantities, spatial directions);
- **clear**, **concise** language.

> Don't introduce more than one of these structural or language features at a time.
> Build up children's understanding of the text type gradually.

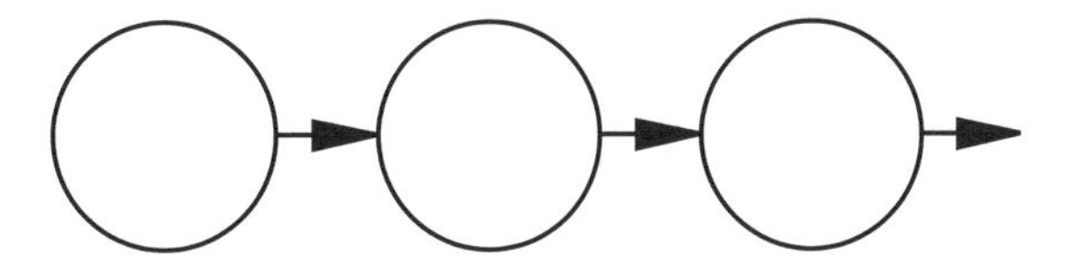

Key teaching points

- Simple instruction text is very direct, and thus fairly easy for young children to write. It is a useful vehicle for demonstrating major differences between the use of language in stories and in factual writing (e.g. descriptive language chosen for clarity, not vividness).
- It can also be used as a vehicle for focusing on verbs, as imperative verbs tend to be up at the front of the sentence. However, since the term 'imperative' is not very memorable for young children, I now use 'bossy verbs' (a term suggested by a Yorkshire teacher).
- It is very helpful if children can actually carry out the process concerned before they write. For this reason cross-curricular links to art, DT, ICT, PE and so on are invaluable.
- Diagrams help make instructions clear. Children also need to be taught how to draw and label simple clear diagrams.

> Common forms of **instruction text**:
>
> - recipe;
> - technical manual (e.g. for car, computer);
> - non-fiction book (e.g. sports skills, art);
> - timetable, route finder;
> - list of rules;
> - posters, notices, signs;
> - sewing or knitting patterns;
> - instructions on packaging (e.g. cooking or washing instructions).

HOW TO MAKE A PERSONAL PHOTO FRAME

You will need:

A good photo of yourself
A rectangle of thick card, bigger than your photo
4 strips of thinner coloured card
Scissors
Glue
Coloured crayons or pens

1. Put the photo of yourself on the thick card, right in the middle. Use a dab of glue to stick it in position.
2. Lay one of the strips of coloured card across the top of your photo. Trim the strip so that it covers the thick card and overlaps the photo a tiny bit.

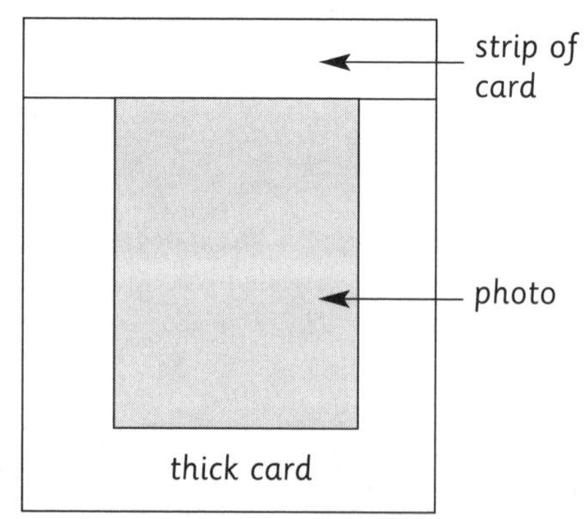

3. Do the same with the other strips to cover the thick card at the bottom and sides of the photo.
4. Glue the four strips together at the corners so they make a frame. Use coloured crayons or pens to decorate it with pictures of things you like.

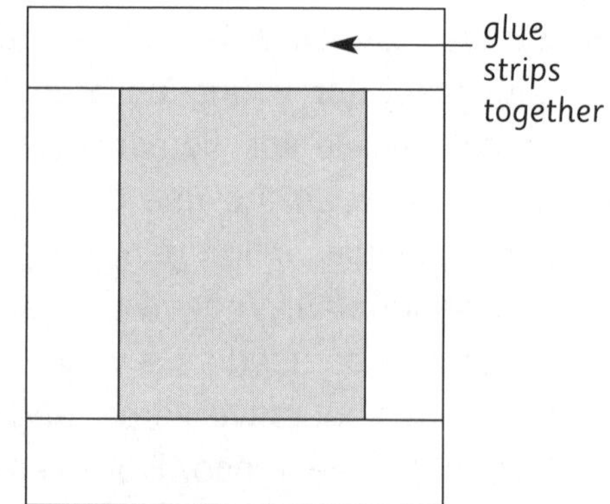

5. Stick the frame over your photo onto the thick card.
6. Put your personal framed photo in the class 'Rogues Gallery'.

Shared reading of 'How to make a personal photo frame'

The passage can be used for one or more of the following, depending on children's age and ability.

Following instructions

The materials for this activity may need a degree of preparation (cutting the backing card and coloured strips to the right size for making the frame). Young children will probably not measure card strips, etc. for themselves, and the space available on a photocopiable A4 page meant we could not provide more detailed instructions.

Read the instructions with the class, then provide the equipment and ask children to follow the instructions to make their photo frames. If you are doing an 'Ourselves' topic, the 'Rogues Gallery' can be integrated with the display.

Introducing flowcharts

Re-read the instructions, then demonstrate how to turn them into a visual flow chart – pictures and memory-jogger notes. Help the children see that instructions are broken down into stages and organised in a time sequence (like the timeline).

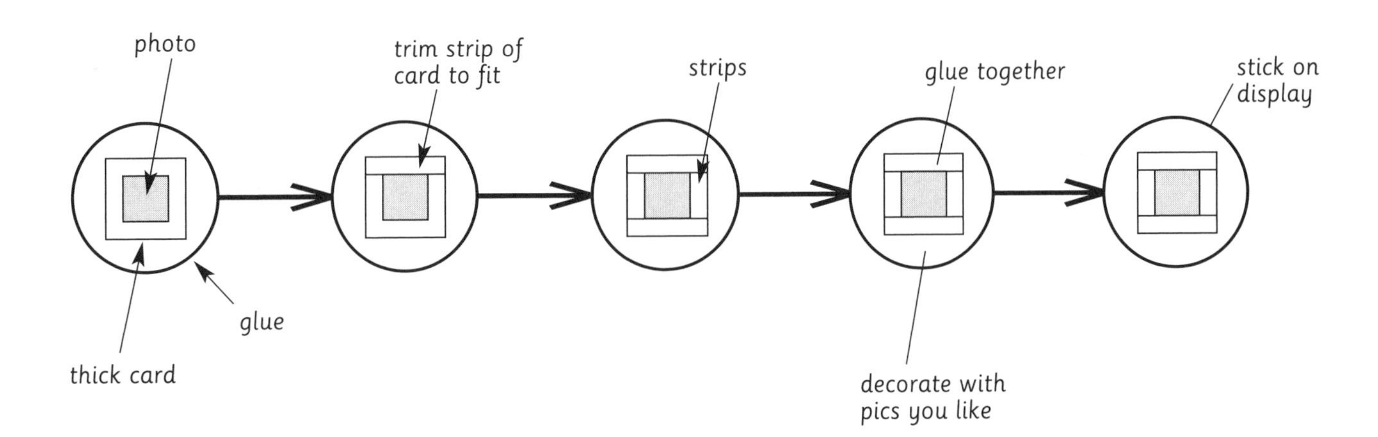

Numbered steps

Remind children about timeline notes for 'true stories', and discuss how the skeleton framework for instructions is similar to and different from the timeline. Establish that either type of writing could be on either framework (since both show events in time order) but the flowchart is more suitable for instructions, as it clearly breaks the process into steps.

Ask pupils to reread the instruction passage, one step each. Discuss why the author has chosen to use numbers to signal the different stages in the process, rather than time connectives, as in a recount. Talk about why he has divided it up in this way: how might he have chosen the number of steps? Could he have made it more or fewer? (Warn children about the danger of splitting the process into too many steps.)

'Bossy' verbs

Cover the first word of each instruction with sticky notes or blank-out tape. Invite pupils to read the sentences, one at a time, and work out what the missing word might be. Reveal the word each time to check. As you work through the text, help the children recognise that these words are all 'doing words'.

Introduce, or revise, the term 'verb' and explain that all sentences have verbs in them. Because instructions are all about telling you what to do, the verbs are very important so they're usually right up at the front of the sentence, 'bossing you about'.

Diagrams and labels

Cover up the captions on the diagrams in the instruction text. Can pupils remember what they say?

Reveal them and discuss why the labels are just words and phrases, rather than complete sentences. Discuss the importance of diagrams, helping children recognise that it is often easier to explain with a very simple labelled picture than in words. Explain that the lines connecting labels to diagrams are called 'leader lines' and should be drawn with a ruler.

Demonstrate how to draw and label a diagram (choose something related to the ongoing work of the class, or something familiar like an item of clothing). Ask pupils in pairs to try drawing a labelled diagram of a similar item.

Position phrases

Return once more to the instruction text. Explain that in craft activities, such as making the photo frame, correct positioning of parts is very important. Ask pupils to read the instructions, one sentence each, looking out for and highlighting phrases which answer the question 'where'. Collect good examples of these on a poster for future reference.

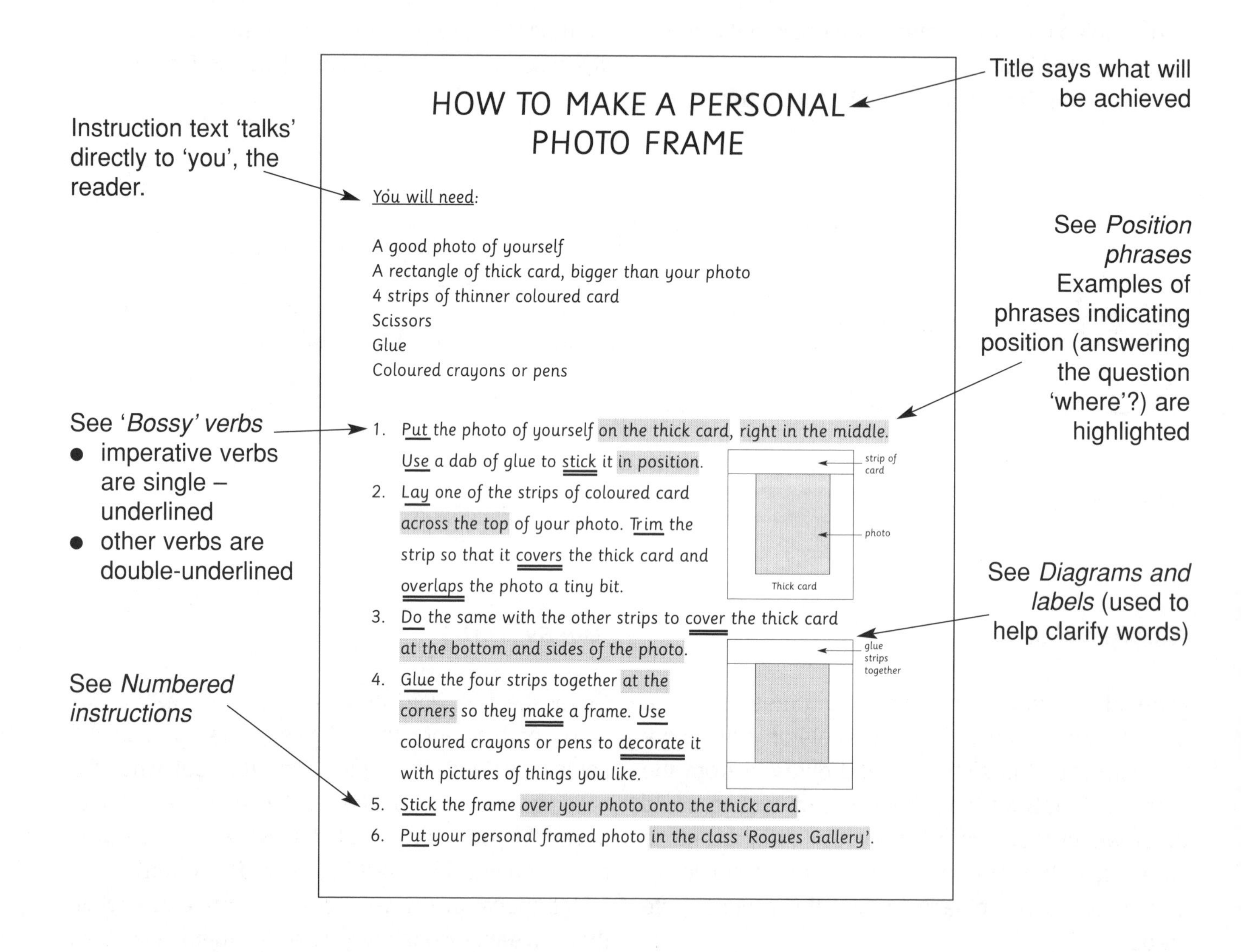

Shared Writing: instructions for craft activity

Lesson 1: talking about instructions

Note: to complete this activity, each child needs half an egg box.

Enlarge the pictures on page 60 to share with the children. Talk about each one, establishing:

- that the first picture gives the list of equipment and the others are steps in the sequence of instructions for making a caterpillar;
- the names of all the items of equipment;
- what the child is doing in each picture;
- that the stapler must be used by an adult.

Let children follow the picture instructions to make caterpillars.

Lesson 2: making memory-jogger instructions

Soon after making the caterpillars, help pupils make flowchart notes of what they did. Do not show the picture instructions.

Start by listing the items needed. Then discuss how you can jot down the first instruction (cutting the egg box in half). Children will probably want to draw it, but demonstrate how it's quicker (and easier) to write: Cut box in half.

Demonstrate and scribe to make flowchart notes for the first three stages.

Talk about bossy verbs and any other sentence level work you have covered through shared reading.

Ask pupils to copy the start of the flowchart, and then make their own notes to complete the instruction flowchart.

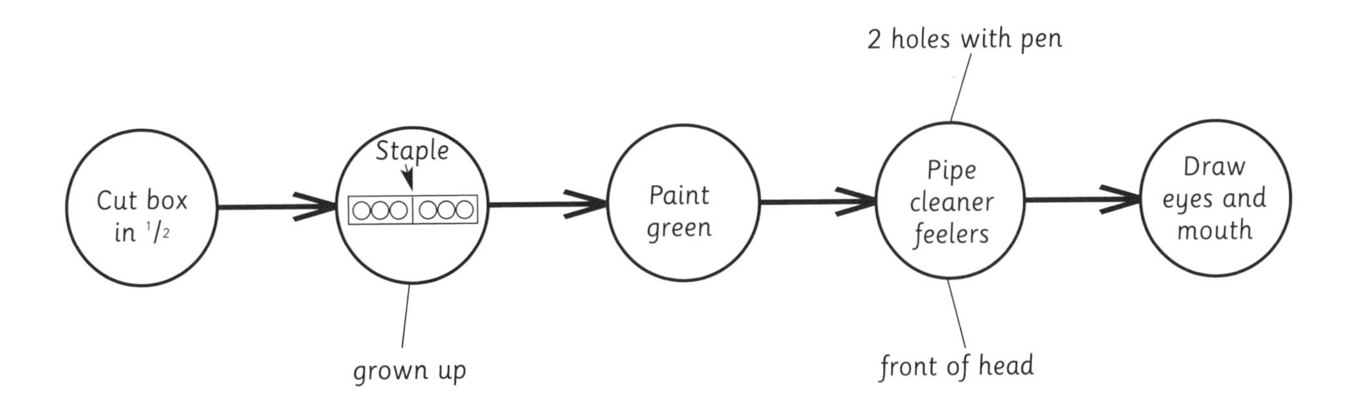

Lesson 3: turning memory-joggers into sentences

Use the visual prompt about instruction organisation on page 33 (in Instruction case studies), to remind pupils of what is involved in writing instructions.

Ask them independently to write a title and list of 'What you need' based on your notes for the last lesson.

When most are ready, model how to use your skeleton notes to write up the first stage or two in the process, using a mixture of demonstration, scribing and supported composition.

Children can then complete the writing of the instructions, in pairs or independently.

Lessons 4: writing instructions independently

Provide materials and spoken directions for pupils to make butterfly pictures by folding paper, painting a 'half-butterfly' on one side of the fold, then pressing the two sides together to make a symmetrical picture.

Ask pupils in pairs to:

- create a list of materials and flowchart notes for the activity;
- use these to write instructions on 'How to make a butterfly picture'.

(The two craft activities suggested here link to the explanation writing activity on page 67.)

How to make a caterpillar

3.4 Explanation text

Purpose: to explain how or why something happens

Text structure

- title often asks a question or defines the process to be explained;
- text usually opens with general statement(s) to introduce the topic;
- a series of logical steps explaining the process, usually in time order often accompanied by **diagram**(s);
- basic skeleton framework – a **flowchart** ('this happens, leading to this, which leads to this', etc.).

Language features

- **present tense** (the process is general);
- **time connectives** and other devices to aid sequential structure;
- **causal connectives** and other devices demonstrating **cause and effect**.

> Don't introduce more than one of these structural or language features at a time.
> Build up children's understanding of the text type gradually.

Key teaching points

- Explanations are very difficult to write, particularly for young children. Before putting pen to paper, children must thoroughly understand the process they are about to explain. Making a skeleton framework first – especially a flowchart and/or labelled diagram – develops understanding. However, the process of developing a suitable skeleton framework can in itself aid understanding.
- The language of explanation is also extremely difficult for many KS1 children, who are just getting to grips with the idea of cause and effect. They need plenty of opportunities to 'play with' words like 'because', 'so', 'unless' and 'if'.

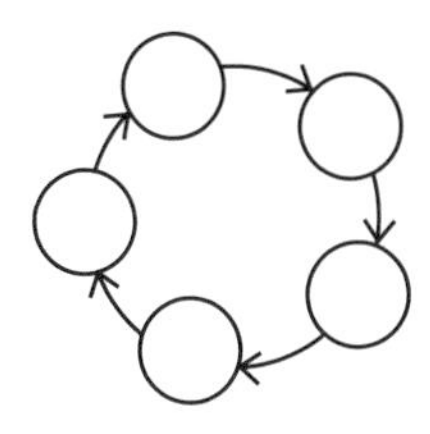

a **cycle**

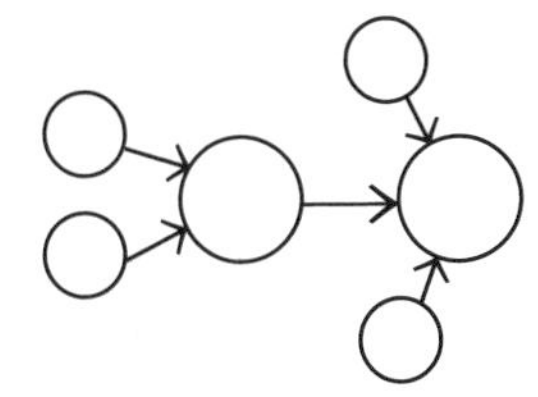

multiple causes and/or effects

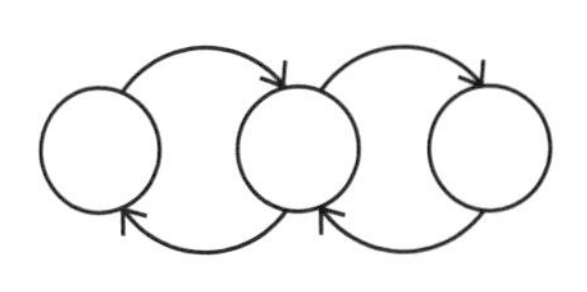

reversible effects

- However, even making the flowchart can be tricky! There are many possible variations, depending upon the process in question.
- Children need to see plenty of models created by the teacher. They also need time to experiment with different ways of representing a process (collaborative work is particularly useful).

> Forms of text which may be **explanation text**
>
> - text book;
> - encyclopaedia entry;
> - non-fiction book (e.g. geography, biology);
> - technical manual (e.g. for car, dishwasher);
> - 'question and answer' articles and leaflets;
> - write-up of science experiment.

HOW DO BABIES GROW?

Newborn babies are very small. Most of them weigh round about 3½ kilograms and are only about 53 centimetres from head to toe. Some are even smaller. However, soon after they are born, babies are ready to eat! Their food is milk, which they suck from their mummy's breast or from a bottle.

The milk helps the baby grow, so by 3 months old it weighs about 6 kilograms and is around 60 centimetres long. Its tummy is growing stronger too. This means mum can give the baby some solid food as well as milk. The food is special mushy baby food because the baby does not have any teeth, so it cannot chew yet.

At 6 months old a baby is about 8 kilograms and 68 centimetres long. Its body is stronger now so it can sit up and play. Its little teeth are starting to come through. This means it can have some hard food like rusks as well as baby food and milk.

By one year old, most babies weigh around 9½ kilograms and measure about 72 cms. They can stand up, and will soon start to walk. They usually have several teeth, so they can eat the same food as older children, as long as it is cut up small. As they eat more and more, they will grow heavier, taller and stronger.

Shared reading of 'How do babies grow?'

The passage can be used for one or more of the following, depending on children's age and ability.

Introducing flowcharts

Read the passage and demonstrate how to turn it into a flowchart. Help pupils see that each paragraph deals with the baby's development at a particular age, which become the stage in the sequence (a circle). Details about the baby at each stage can be added around the circle, as in a report spidergram.

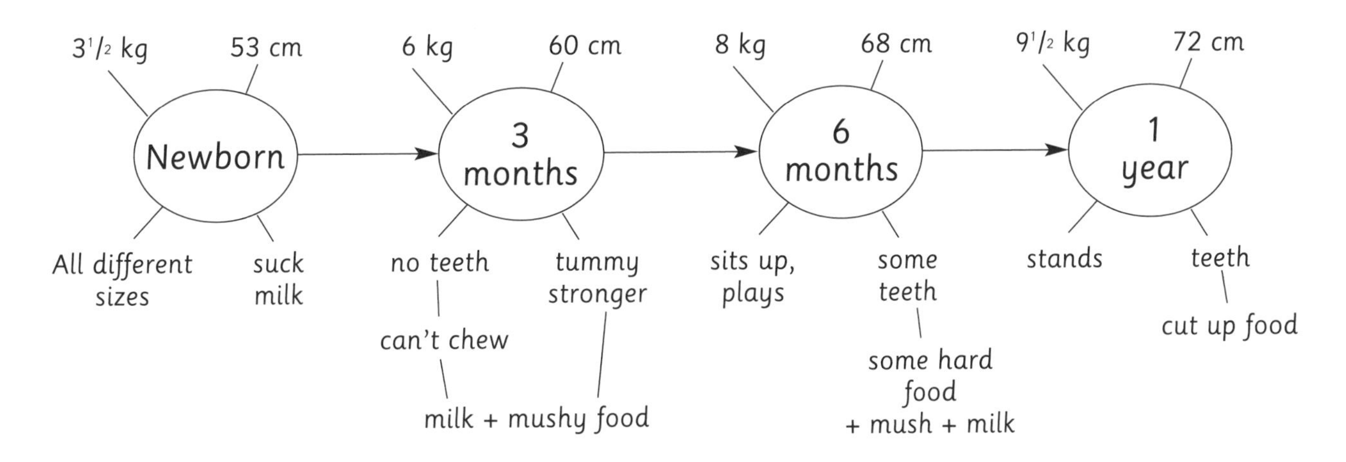

Cause and effect

Many children have difficulty with the language of cause and effect, and visual representations can be helpful in clarifying the concept. Talk about simple examples of cause and effect that are familiar to the children and represent them in skeleton form, e.g.

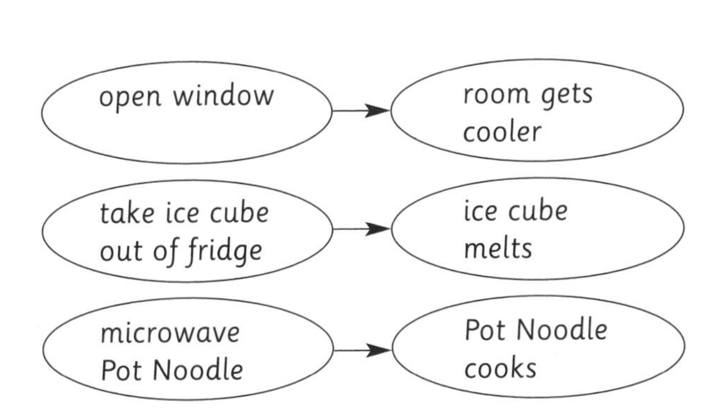

Discuss which is the cause and which is the effect in each case. Label them 'C' and 'E'.

Now introduce these speaking frames, and help the children work out how to fit each cause and effect into each frame.

When __________, __________

__________ so ___________

__________. This means that___________.

_______________________because_________.

The reason that __________ is that__________.

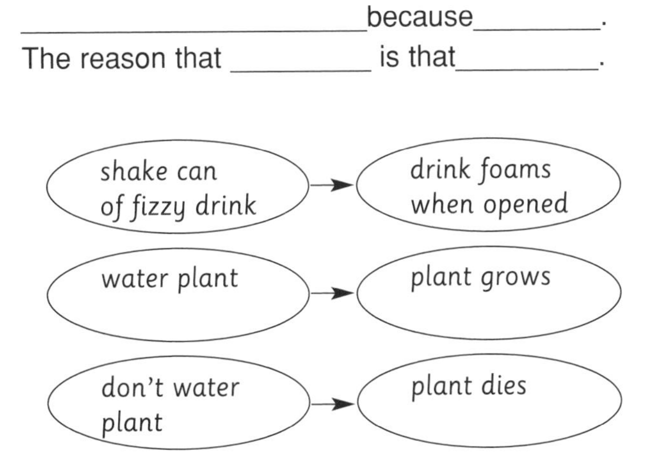

Help the children see that, in the last two frames, the effect is mentioned before the cause.

Reread the passage, looking out for and collecting examples of causal language. In each case, make a diagram like the ones above to show the cause and effect. One sentence contains two cause and effect constructions:

Explanation text is usually written in the present tense

HOW DO BABIES GROW?

Newborn babies are very small. Most of them weigh round about 3½ kilograms and are only about 53 centimetres from head to toe. Some are even smaller. However, soon after they are born, babies are ready to eat! Their food is milk, which they suck from their mummy's breast or from a bottle.

The milk helps the baby grow, so by 3 months old it weighs about 6 kilograms and is around 60 centimetres long. Its tummy is growing stronger too. This means mum can give the baby some solid food as well as milk. The food is special mushy baby food because the baby does not have any teeth, so it cannot chew yet.

At 6 months old a baby is about 8 kilograms and 68 centimetres long. Its body is stronger now so it can sit up and play. Its little teeth are starting to come through. This means it can have some hard food like rusks as well as baby food and milk.

By one year old, most babies weigh around 9½ kilograms and measure about 72 cms. They can stand up, and will soon start to walk. They usually have several teeth, so they can eat the same food as older children, as long as it is cut up small. As they eat more and more, they will grow heavier, taller and stronger.

See *Cause and effect*
Examples of causal language are underlined

See *Organising ideas*
Highlighted section give patterned information

See *General information*
Examples of words and phrases suggesting babies are all slightly different are wriggly-underlined

See *Singular or plural*
Second and third paragraphs are written in the 'generalised singular'

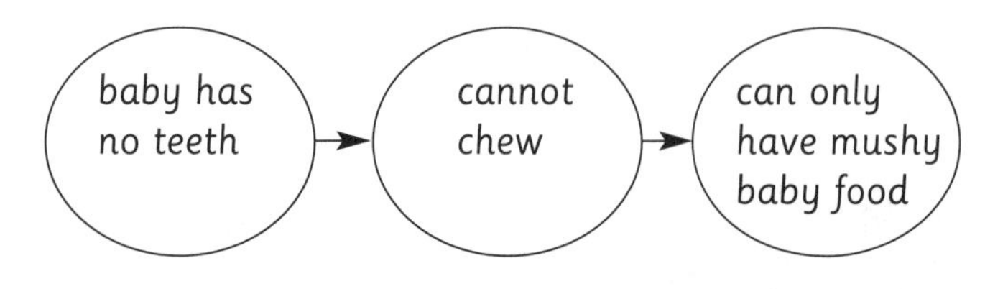

Organising ideas

Ask some pupils to reread the passage, one paragraph each. Can they see:

- why the author has chosen to put the paragraph breaks where they are?
- a pattern in the way each paragraph is constructed (age, weight and length of baby; development and diet)?

Collect the four constructions giving information about age, weight and length (highlighted) and help children see that the author has tried to vary the way he presents these facts. Can pupils think of other ways of presenting the information each time (e.g. 'When the baby is ...', 'Three months later, the baby weighs ... ').

Singular or plural

Before re-reading the passage again, ask pupils whether the information is about babies in general or one baby in particular. How do they know this? (The usual answer is something like 'Because it says *babies*, not *baby*'.)

Ask some children to read the passage, a sentence each to check whether this is true. Discuss the fact that the middle two paragraphs are actually written in the singular. This use of the 'generalised singular' can be confusing to young children. The technique allows writers to vary sentence construction (repetition of *babies* would become boring). However, it can lead to problems with gender (the use of 'it' here sounds slightly odd, but a generalised baby does not have a gender, and repeated use of 'he' or 'she' would make sentences too complex for young readers).

Look in other non-fiction books for examples of this frequently used device e.g. ('The snail ... ', 'The caterpillar ... ') and ensure children are not under the impression that these are specific snails, caterpillars, etc.

General information

Another difficulty for authors writing generalised information (e.g. reports and explanations) is that any descriptive detail must refer to an 'average': there will be variation between different examples of the 'specimens' under consideration. This means they need to convey the possibility of variation.

Ask some children to read the passage, a sentence each, checking for words and phrases that suggest that not all babies are the same (see wiggly underlining) and make a collection of these for future reference.

Keep an eye open for this type of language used in other report and explanation texts you read across the curriculum.

Shared Writing: how butterflies grow

Lesson 1: making skeleton notes

Enlarge the pictures on page 67 to share with the children. Talk about each one, establishing what is happening at each stage in the butterfly's development.

Help the children create an explanation flowchart, e.g.

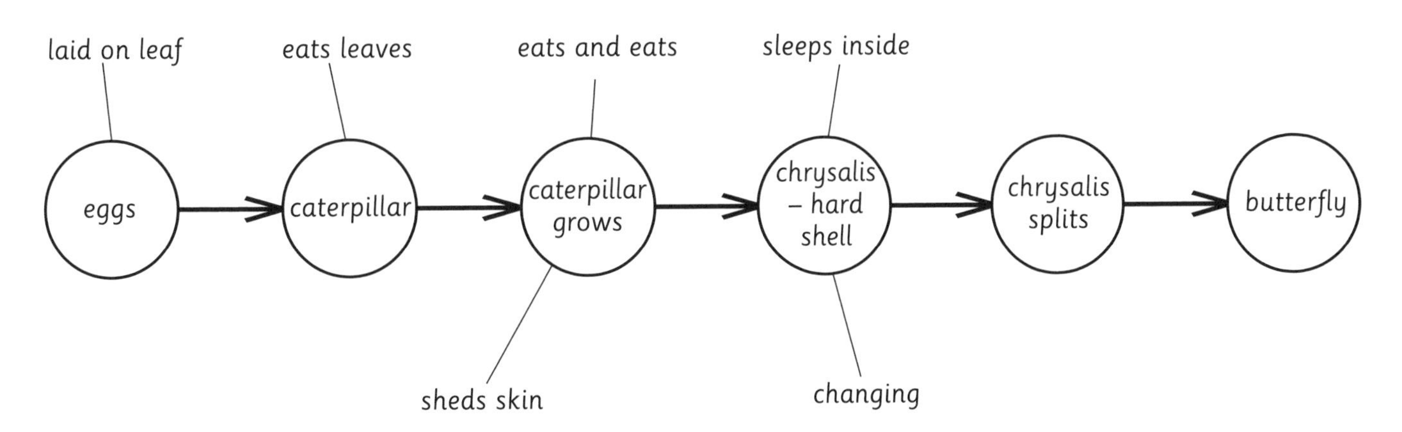

Establish that the adult butterfly is now able to lay more eggs, so the whole process begins again. Show how, in such a case, the flowchart can be converted into a cycle model:

laid on leaf
eggs
eats leaves
caterpillar
eats and eats
caterpillar grows
sheds skin
chrysalis – hard shell
sleeps inside
changing
chrysalis splits
butterfly

Lesson 2: turning memory-joggers into sentences

Model how to use your skeleton notes to write up:

- the first stage in the process;
- the beginning of the second stage.

Use a mixture of demonstration, scribing and supported composition, and point out features of layout and language covered in earlier lessons.

Children can then complete the writing of the explanation, in pairs or independently.

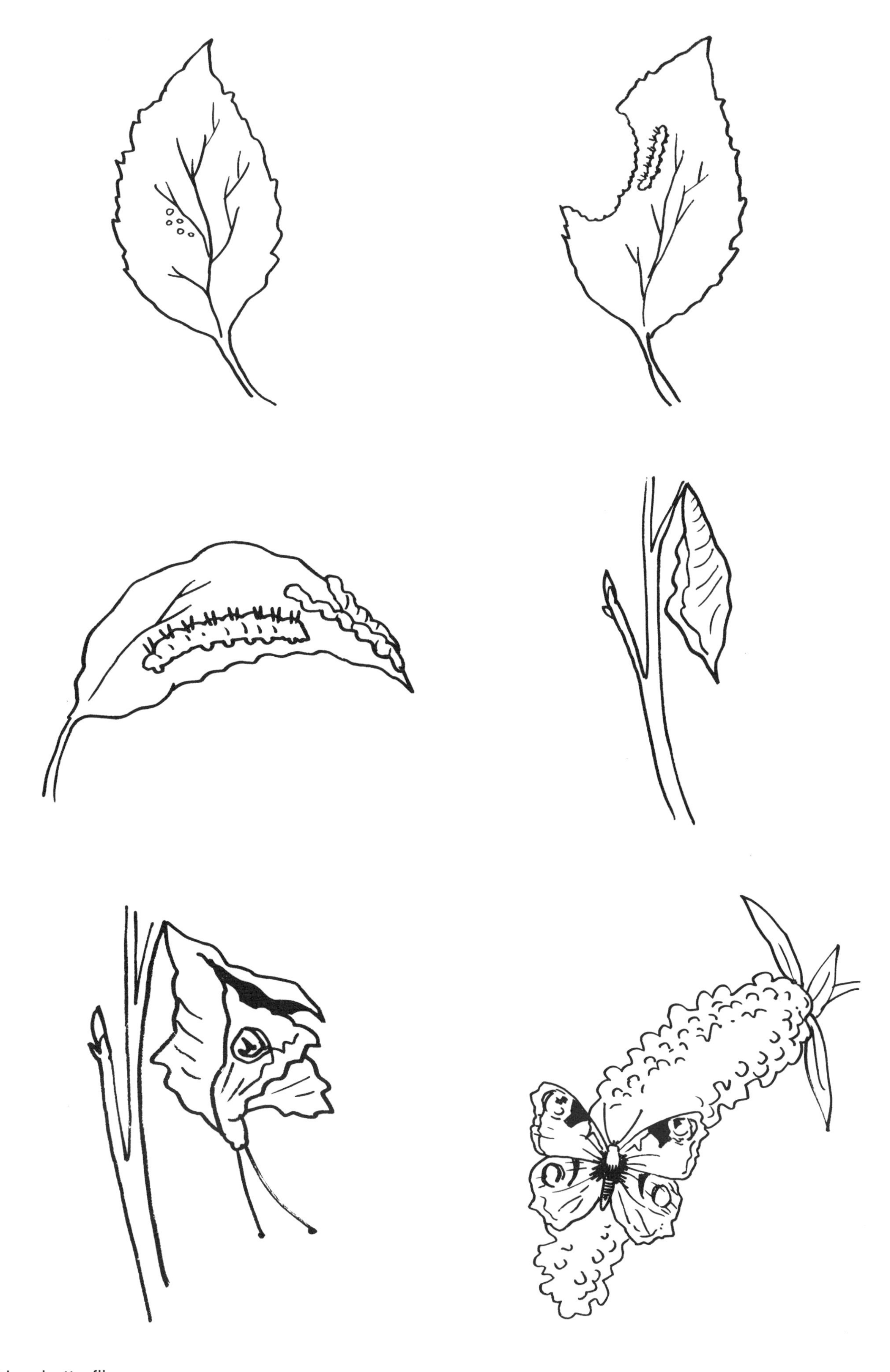

How butterflies grow

PART 4

Appendices

Appendix 1 Nuts and bolts: some suggestions about teaching writing skills

In recent years, there's been lots of attention to the 'nuts and bolts' skills involved in writing and the best ways to teach them. And there's no doubt that, in the early stages, children's ability to write is underpinned by their level of skill in phonics, spelling and handwriting.

Some lucky children pick up these sub-skills fairly easily, usually because they come from families where they've been sung, read and talked to since birth, and their parents have unconsciously modelled literate behaviour to them almost every day of their lives. They soon start using 'experimental writing' in their play, and – given the occasional hint and helping hand – can develop their skills informally. But the majority need a great deal of structured, systematic teaching to help them 'put words down on paper'.

The key task for teachers is to decide when and how to intervene:

- to support children at their own level when they're attempting to write;
- to teach phonic, spelling and handwriting skills formally, to ability groups and – in the later stages – to the whole class.

After 15 years of involvement in early years literacy, I'm now convinced that we shouldn't put children under any pressure to write independently until they are at least six – and even then we should tread very carefully. This opinion is now shared by many authorities on literacy and early years, although at the time of writing most UK government offices haven't quite caught up with it. (However, Wales has instituted a Foundation Phase between 3 and 7, modelled on successful Scandinavian practice, which looks very hopeful. There's a Teacher's TV video clip about it on You Tube: http://www.teachers.tv/video/12133).

Foundations of Literacy, 3rd edition (Network Continuum, 2008), written with my early years colleague Ros Bayley, provides many examples of the sorts of play-based activities that can lay sound foundations for literacy teaching, without involving formal lessons in reading and writing until children are six or seven. One vital element in this early practice is the creation of a language-rich environment, with plenty of opportunities for children to talk, hear stories, and watch adults modelling literate behaviour, in the same way that the 'lucky' children described above have imbibed literacy at their parents' knees.

Phonics

Why, when and how?

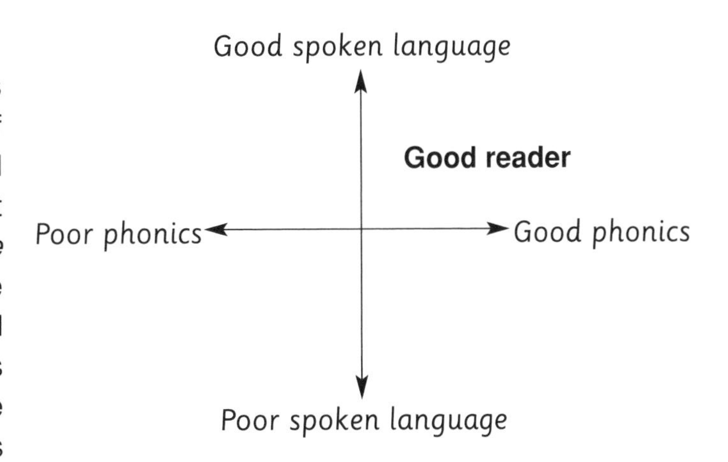

In terms of classroom practice, most debate in recent years has centred around the teaching of phonics. This diagram is based on the work of Dr Morag Stuart in the Appendix to the *Rose Report* of 2006. It shows the interrelationship between rapid 'word recognition' (which means the ability to rapidly synthesise an unfamiliar word from its phonetic elements: /b/ /a/ /sh/ → 'bash') and language comprehension (implicit in the level of children's command of spoken language). If children have good phonics skills and good spoken language they will, almost inevitably, be good readers.

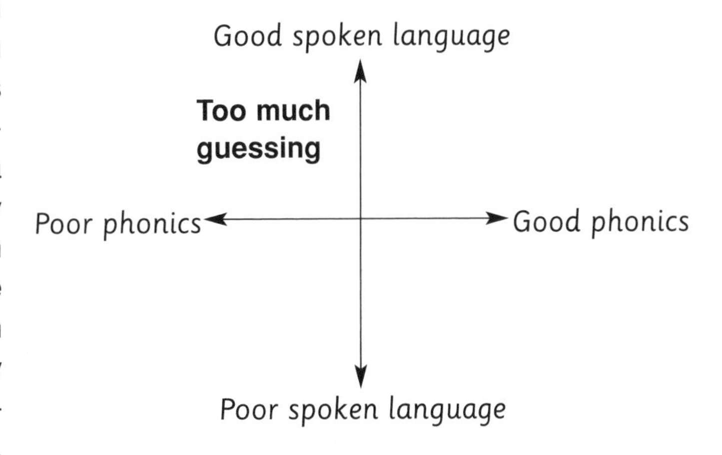

However, those children with good command of spoken language but poor phonics skills often fall into the trap of guessing unknown words. This is not a great handicap in the early stages as a bright child can usually make pretty effective guesses, but as time goes on and the level of vocabulary becomes more difficult, guessing doesn't work. Unfortunately, a child who has learned to guess usually finds it very difficult to slow down his or her brain sufficiently to acquire the skills of decoding.

Children whose ability to discriminate phonemes is impaired for physiological reasons find it difficult to learn phonics, and – if their spoken language is good – often become inveterate guessers. By the time these children reach seven or eight they're usually identified as 'dyslexic'.

Very few children have a genetic predisposition to dyslexia. However, if phonics is taught badly or sketchily (or not taught at all), children with no physiological difficulties may also learn to guess, and thus be unwilling to slow down their brains at a later date to learn to decode – we could call this 'acquired dyslexia'. It's likely that, when phonics fell out of favour in the latter part of the twentieth century, many children – especially boys – suffered from acquired dyslexia. So to avoid the artificial creation of reading problems, we have to ensure that children are taught phonics, and taught it well, before being asked to read and write.

On the other hand, if a child has poor spoken language but has been trained in phonic decoding, he or she will be able to decode but without comprehension. As it's impossible truly to 'read' or 'write' a text without simultaneously attending to both phonics and

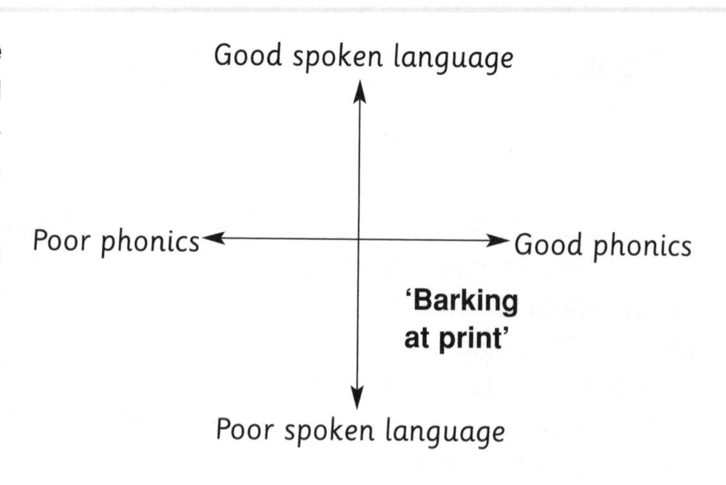

meaning, this child will struggle in literacy lessons and will usually lose interest in the activity. This used to happen regularly before the 1970s, when children were 'trained' in basic phonics without much attention to meaning. The children concerned were said to be 'barking at print' when they read, and struggled with writing throughout their school careers.

Indeed, it was because so many children from less advantaged homes were found to be 'barking at print' that confidence in phonics as a teaching method waned, and phonics was all but abandoned in the late 1970s for around 20 years. There is a strong possibility that, unless we concentrate on the development of speaking and listening skills as well as phonics, these children will again fail to make adequate progress in reading.

In Scotland, where several local authorities have taught systematic synthetic phonics for several years, many 11-year-olds from disadvantaged homes do not progress beyond a nine-year-old reading level, even on a phonic test – i.e. they are not independent readers. (Interestingly, children who started school early and were thus subjected to phonics teaching from the age of four often do not even attain nine-year-old levels of competence by their eleventh year – as one headteacher put it 'they seem to be inevitably among the failures').

Good spoken language

Poor phonics — Good phonics

Potential special needs

Poor spoken language

The most comprehensive failures, of course, are the children who have neither well-developed spoken language nor phonic skill. During their nursery and early education, they need:

- plenty of real-life interaction and fun to develop their oral language skills;
- lots of 'natural' opportunities to acquire phonological and phonemic awareness (learning songs, rhymes, and rhythmic alliterative jingles that alert them to the sounds of language).

Otherwise, they may well go through their primary school career with 'special needs', and experience has shown that 'catch-up programmes' are not wildly successful.

If practitioners are aware of this complex relationship between phonics (including phonological and phonemic awareness) and proficiency in spoken language, they can during the early years use their professional judgement about the level and type of phonics teaching appropriate for particular children. Songs, rhymes and jingles are usually fun for all young children at all stages of development, but specific phonics teaching is unlikely to have much effect until a child begins consciously to play with language of his or her own volition. Practitioners need to listen out for:

- delighted independent repetition of particular songs and/or rhymes;
- spontaneous rhyming (e.g. 'This is Mr Ooly Pooly Dooly');
- other spontaneous language play (e.g. making up their own repetitive rhythmic chants).

Once children show interest in playing with language in this way, they're usually ready for more specific directed attention to phonics – oral games like:

- I Spy (using phonemes rather than letters, e.g something beginning with '*cuh*');
- listening for their own names in phonemic segments (e.g. 'This person can go and get his coat first: '/j/ /ai/ /k/. OK, now it's /b/ /e/ /th/ /a/ /n/ /y/.');
- playing the robot game ('What word is the robot saying? /d/ /o/ /g/').

If they've also been used to seeing environmental print around the classroom, watching the teacher write, and singing an alphabet song (while looking at an alphabet chart), they should soon be ready to start linking the letter-sounds to the letters. There are now many commercial courses available for systematic teaching of phonics.

But of course it's highly unlikely that all children will reach this stage at the same time. So phonics teaching should be aimed at groups, not the whole class, and children who lag behind need plenty of individual attention at the appropriate level.

Phonics in writing development

In any class of five- or six-year-olds, there may be children at each of the following developmental levels in terms of writing:

- random scribble;
- scribble that looks like writing;
- individual shapes that look like letters;
- some real letters used randomly (especially letters from own name);
- letters and shapes written from left to right across the page;
- individual letters used to represent words (usually initial sounds);
- more than one letter used to represent a word (usually significant consonant;
- sounds; in CVC words the first and last letters);
- some CVC words and key sight words spelled correctly (use of medial vowel in CVC words);
- simple regular words and key sight words usually spelled correctly.

The following examples of writing (in response to hearing the story of Goldilocks) are all from the same class. Suggestions for helping each child are given alongside, bearing in mind that:

- on the one hand, we don't want to put them off forever by too heavy-handed support;
- on the other, if we wait for writing to happen 'naturally', there's a good chance it never will.

This child does not yet understand that pictures are different from writing or that letters are symbols rather than images. She needs to learn, through experience, that writing is a tool for communication, and that words are stable and read the same however often you read them, e.g. through:

- being read to every day;
- being in a print-rich environment, where labels and other print provide information of interest and relevance to the child;
- learning to recognise her own name and that of others;
- seeing the teacher write regularly (e.g. Shared Writing of labels or brief captions).

She also needs to build up her phonological awareness and auditory memory in preparation for reading and writing through:

- lots of singing and other musical activities;
- being encouraged to join in with stories;
- repeated hearing of rhymes, and encouragement to learn simple rhymes by heart.

This child has used recognisable letters that do not correspond to the phonemes in the words (he's probably been trained to write these letters on birthday cards or presents, but without any understanding of the phonic code). Specific teaching should focus developing appreciation of simple sound–symbol correspondences, e.g.:

- general phonological awareness activities and phonic play;
- systematic fun introduction of phonic sounds (e.g. *Jolly Phonics*) along with other children at about the same level;
- games for developing awareness of initial sounds;
- simple blending and segmenting games, to ensure he doesn't become fixated on initial sounds.

This child has heard and written a symbol to represent the initial phoneme in each word, but has left no spaces between the words. She needs:

'Get out of my house!'

- systematic teaching of sound–symbol correspondences, ensuring coverage of one way to write each phoneme;
- fun activities for blending and segmenting of words (oral games and opportunities to build words with letter-cards, magnetic letters, etc);
- games to sensitise her to final sounds in words (e.g. using a puppet that 'can't say the final sound');
- help in recognising the spaces between words, and specific attention to this during Shared Writing (e.g. remembering to put 'finger-spaces');
- opportunities to write, as part of play and to record her own thoughts and experiences, and lots of interest in what she produces.

This child has discerned and represented the initial, final and medial phonemes in each word, but has not heard the 'n' of 'don't'. There are no spaces between the words and directionality may not be secure. Specific phonics teaching should focus on:

- systematic teaching of more advanced phonic knowledge, including blending and segmenting of CCVC and CVCC words;
- help to notice the spaces between the words.

However, while this child is clearly ahead of his peers in phonic knowledge, there is a real problem with handwriting. This shows the dangers of concentrating on one writing sub-skill at the expense of the others. If a child's ability to recognise and remember sounds seriously outruns the ability to transcribe them, he or she may end up with 'special educational needs' as serious as those of the unfortunate children who can't link phonics and meaning.

It's therefore sensible in the early stages to teach **phonics for reading** without expecting children to write the letters. They can learn to build words, and even whole sentences, using letter-cards, magnetic or wooden letters, phonix cubes or other concrete aids. Some children who catch on quickly to the code – like the boy who wrote the final example – may also enjoy writing on the computer.

Meanwhile, the second strand of 'nuts and bolts' teaching is the development of the physical skills required for fluent writing.

Handwriting

Moving into writing

It takes a long time for a small child – especially a boy! – to develop the physical control and coordination required to sit at a desk and write. So early years practice must involve lots of opportunities for movement through:

- self-chosen active play, particularly outdoors;
- smaller-scale play-based activities, such as making things, puppetry or sit-down games involving motor control;
- patterned activities, such as action songs, PE and dancing;
- opportunities for mark-making in various ways, including drawing and painting;
- activities involving hand-eye coordination, such as using tools, threading, jigsaws and so on.

The significance of early movement in children's literacy development should never be underestimated, and is one of the reasons that education in the years up to six or seven should be essentially play-based.

Once children have reasonable control of bodily movement and hand–eye coordination, the key to good handwriting is sound letter formation, based in three key letter-strokes:

- the 'c' shape (starting at the top) that underlies 'c', 'a', 'd', 'g', 'o', 'q' and 's';
- the downward stroke involved in 'l', 't', 'i', 'u' and 'y';
- the upward curve required for 'r', 'n', 'm', 'h', 'p' and 'b'.

This does not mean worksheets! Physical activity is still very important, so children need to start with large-scale motor movements: writing with a stick or finger in the sand-tray; using paints, chalks or big felt pens to make colourful collages (a cabbage leaf full of curly caterpillar 'c' shapes, for instance); and sky-writing the shapes, using their whole arm, right from the shoulder. There are many inspired activities in the programme *Write Dance* by Ragnhild Oussoren (Sage Publications), which in Holland is used between the ages of five and eight.

Linking handwriting to phonics

If they take part in plenty of 'movement for writing', by the time they've mastered basic phonics children should be ready to link the two sub-skills. For some under-sixes (generally girls) this happens naturally, and all that's required of the teacher is occasional nudges to ensure they form letters correctly (rather than getting into bad habits that might hold them up later).

However, I'm now convinced that formal systematic teaching of handwriting should wait until children are six or even seven. It can then be used as an opportunity to revise phonic knowledge already covered for reading, making use of the kinaesthetic learning channel to help children internalise the letter-shapes that go with the sounds.

Again, skywriting and other large-scale practice is best to start with:

- introduce each letter with big movements from the shoulder, using the whole arm;
- next move to finger-writing in the air;
- when the children have the hand-control to do it confidently, they can write on wide-lined paper or whiteboards. (Lines are important because so much about handwriting is to do with letters' orientation to the line.)

Always demonstrate letters so that children see the movements from the right direction – indeed, since this means turning your back on the class, it's usually better if you don't demonstrate yourself. Ask another adult (or a competent child) to stand at the front and demonstrate sky-writing then board-writing the letter, as you describe the movement. This also frees you up to watch how the children are coping, and to move among them, helping to adjust arm-movements as they copy the demonstrator.

Dealing with difficulties

If some children lag behind the others in motor control, let them join in with the large-scale movements only (they can continue to use magnetic letters or the computer when the others write), and provide plenty of opportunities for manipulative play (lacing, threading, cut-and-stick, construction toys, etc.) to develop hand–eye coordination. Ensure these children get extra help to catch up with handwriting as their motor skills develop.

Identify left-handed children as soon as possible. If children are undecided about handedness, try to guide them towards the right-hand, as it will make their lives infinitely easier – but genuine left-handers will show a marked partiality which should be respected. Give extra help, modelling all practice movements and letter formations again for them using your own left hand (do this well away from the rest of the class!).

Keep an eye open for children who hold their pencils awkwardly. If possible, establish correct pencil grip from the moment children begin to use pencils for drawing and tracing. For those who can't remember the best way to hold the pencil, provide a commercial pencil gripper (such as a Stetro grip) for guidance.

Putting it into practice

In Shared Writing demonstrate how to put this knowledge to use in writing words and sentences. Choose sentences that include the sounds/letters of the moment, and give a running commentary as you use phonics and letter-formation to create words and sentences. Ask the class to have a go at a (carefully-selected) word or phrase themselves, using individual wipe-clean whiteboards – these are great for practising letters, because it doesn't matter if you make a mistake. As they become more competent, give an occasional sentence as a dictation – this allows children to concentrate just on hearing the sounds and producing the letters, without the added burden of composition.

Linking handwriting, phonics and spelling

As phonics teaching progresses, use handwriting to mirror the phonic units you introduce – where two letters stand for one phoneme, teach them as a joined unit so that visual and kinaesthetic learning reinforce the idea of the digraph. Treating digraphs (two letters standing for one sound) and trigraphs (three letters standing for one sound) as handwriting units provides a powerful cognitive link when children are spelling out words phoneme by phoneme, e.g.:

ch ee oo air

It also prepares the way for further joining of words as pupils' fluency develops. For instance, it is very helpful to use joined writing for some high frequency irregular words too, to reinforce the fact that these words should be remembered as wholes. Children can usually learn to write 'the' as a whole word quite easily, and it is then a small step to writing 'they' as a whole. The spelling of 'they' creates difficulties for many children, and early establishment of a kinaesthetic model of the word would be helpful.

he → the → they

High frequency words can be taught in this way in groups as children's hand control develops:

he the my or come
she they you for some
me there your

one was said from are
done want
gone

As children's reading skills progress, they move from phoneme-by-phoneme spelling to processing words in larger chunks (such as onset and rime, e.g. ch-air, str-eam). This can be reflected in handwriting terms by increasingly treating common letter strings as joined units e.g.:

ing and all old

As you teach children how to join more and more letter strings and words, you can encourage them to use the same joins in their own writing.

Handwriting and spelling can continue to go hand in hand as pupils' skills increase. Short snappy lessons are best, each concentrating on a group of words with similar sound and/or spelling pattern. This is an ideal opportunity to revise and review phonic knowledge and high frequency words. Short dictations featuring familiar words are also very valuable, as they allow children to concentrate just on spelling and handwriting, without worrying about what to write.

Handwriting practice

Older children also need occasional opportunities to concentrate exclusively on handwriting, to practise joins, neatness and fluency. Patterns can be helpful, and sentences featuring all the letters of the alphabet (such as 'The quick brown fox jumps over the lazy dog') are useful copybook exercises. With your help, children can make up more examples for themselves. They will also benefit from occasional copying of favourite poems or other extracts.

Handwriting comfort

When writing, a child's feet should be comfortably on the ground and his/her forearm resting on the table. The non-writing hand should rest on the paper to steady it. Seat left-handers so the movement of their arm does not clash with the right arm movement of a right-handed child. All children should have a clear view of the board on which letter formation is demonstrated, and should not have to twist in their seat to watch or copy.

Spelling

Sadly, English is only phonetically regular up to a point – and many of the most common words in the language are phonetically irregular. Correct spelling depends on the orchestration of auditory, visual and kinaesthetic memory, and the suggestions in 'Handwriting' above show how these links can be made from the very beginning.

From the age of six or seven, teaching spelling is about alerting children to language **patterns**:

- patterns of sounds and letters, such as onset and rime;
- patterns relating to grammatical function, such as common suffixes;
- patterns relating to word origins, such as the link between *sign* and *signal.*

In order to study words in this way, we have to take them out of context, which means devoting a little time, preferably every day, to teaching spelling by **eye, ear, hand and brain.**

Traditional workbook exercises, wordlists and spelling tests are not enough. Mastery of the English spelling system requires the marshalling of sensory information through visual, auditory and kinaesthetic channels. So children need explicit interactive teaching which draws their attention to the shape and sounds of words, the letter patterns within them, and the various ways they can remember these patterns:

- **by eye**: e.g. looking for common letter-groups (such as double letters, or 'sandwiches' like 'ere'); remembering unexpected letters (like the 'o' in the middle of *people*); spotting words within words (such as 'die' in *soldier*) and highlighting the tricky bits of words in a different colour;
- **by ear**: e.g. remembering rhyming groups or pairs (like *come, some*); pronouncing silent letters (as in ***Wed**-nes-day*); reciting tricky spellings in a rhythmic way ('Mrs D, Mrs I, Mrs FFI, Mrs C, Mrs U, Mrs LTY');
- **by hand**: e.g. learning common spelling patterns as joined units, as described in 'Handwriting'; practising joined writing of tricky words over and over again (on paper, or as skywriting, or using a water pistol or a sparkler ...);
- **by brain**: e.g. learning common rules (such as dropping the final 'e' before adding *–ing*, or when to change 'y' to 'i'); memorising or making up mnemonics ('Does Olive Eat Sausages?'); recognising words with related meanings (such as *one, once* and *only*).

Teaching sessions need not take long – the secret of successful teaching of spelling is 'little and often'. For the teacher it involves:

- drawing up a list of relevant words, especially high-frequency words and ones which have relevance to pupils' current work and interest (this can often be the focus of a 'spelling investigation', where pupils hunt for appropriate words);
- focusing on the specific spelling point (e.g. a grammatical rule, a letter string, some aspect of etymology) so that pupils clearly understand the pattern;
- concentrating on some significant words from the list, drawing on – and thus revising – a range of strategies for learning and remembering spellings;
- creating opportunities for pupils to practise recently-learned words in context – short dictation passages provide an opportunity for them to focus just on transcription skills, without the added burden of composition.

Supporting the poor speller

Spelling is an area where differentiation is particularly important. There are always some children whose phonic knowledge lags behind the rest, and others who are just not very good at spelling. They can be involved along with the rest of the class in learning spelling strategies, preferably focusing on commonly misspelled high frequency words, but teachers should exercise judgement on how much to expect of them.

It might sometimes be better to let them work on an individualised programme appropriate to their own level. There are a number of interactive computer courses, such as *Wordshark*, which provide very structured help, but poor spellers really need specialised teaching. The solution to the knotty problem of providing it will necessarily be up to individual teachers in individual schools, with the involvement of the Special Needs teacher.

Have A Go!

No matter how devotedly teachers teach spelling, getting children to remember rules and strategies during their Independent Writing is another matter. Indeed, for novice writers with so many sub-skills to rally, it can be just about impossible. So children need to know that:

- when writing, the most important thing is to get your meaning across;
- you shouldn't lose your thread by worrying unduly about spelling words;
- the answer is to Have A Go at spellings as you write …;
- then come back at the end and check them.

It's worth taking time to establish the Have A Go ethic, by:

- putting up a poster (see next page) and reminding children about it every time they write;
- modelling it regularly during Shared Writing (always remember to spell a few words wrongly, then 'notice' them as you read through and model the best way to find the correct spelling).

Ways of finding the correct spelling include:

- writing the word in various ways until you spot the right one;
- checking in a personal spelling dictionary or a class list of common words;
- asking a good speller (preferably not the teacher if she's busy);
- typing the word into a computer and using the spellchecker, or using an electronic spellchecker.

Most children under eight find it difficult to locate words in a dictionary, so this is an option for the most able spellers only.

The main problem with a Have A Go! ethos is the least able spellers. Children with very poor spelling skills may misspell the same words over and over again (e.g. writing *sed* instead of *said*) and this brings the very real problem that they'll 'over-learn' the misspellings. It is intensely frustrating for a child if the mismatch between what he wants to write and what he's capable of writing is too great, and this can lead to a downward spiral of poor motivation, lack of application and – all too often – deteriorating behaviour patterns.

In terms of spelling, one answer is to provide the child with a 'spelling mat' (see pages 82–83). This is a laminated A3 card on which irregularly misspelled key words are provided in alphabetical lists, and which the child can lean on to write. As the card is laminated, a section for 'Topic words' means that the teacher can provide specific words of the moment and rub them out when no longer required.

Poor spellers can then Have A Go like the rest of the class … unless the word is on the mat. If it's on the mat, they copy it, thus hopefully 'over-learning' the correct spelling.

a	b	c	d	e	f	g	h	i	j
about	back	call	did		first	girl	half		jump
after	ball	called	do		for	go	have		just
again	be	came	don’t		from	going	help		
all	because	can’t	door			good	her		
another	been	come	down				here		
away	boy	could					home		
	brother						house		
	by						how		

t	u	v	w	x	y	z
take	us	very	want		you	
than	under		water		your	
that			way			
their			were			
them			what			
there			when			
these			where			
three			who			
time			will			
too			with			
took			would			
two			was			
they						

TOPIC WORDS

k	l	m	n	o	p	q	r	s
	last	made	name	of	people		ran	said
	laugh	make	new	off	push		right	saw
	like	many	next	old	pull			school
	little	may	night	once	put			see
	live	more	not	one				seen
	lived	much	now	or				she
	love	must		our				should
				out				sister
				over				so
								some

Grammar and punctuation

Once children have begun to grasp these 'word level' skills, they must also begin to develop awareness of the grammatical elements involved in writing. This means learning another layer of sub-skills, concerned with the construction and punctuation of sentences, and ways of varying language use for different purposes.

Children don't need to know what sentences are in order to produce them in speech. But they do need to know in order to **write** them, to punctuate them and gradually to increase their control over ways of constructing them to express and explore their ideas. In the same way, awareness of basic word classes is totally unnecessary for speech, but helpful for understanding spelling rules, like adding '-ed' and '-ing' to verbs. And knowing a range of words for connecting ideas together can help move children away from the perennial '*and then ... and then ... and then*' of spoken language.

However, as outlined in 'Talk for Writing' (page 9), it's not necessary to go into detailed explanations. Neither do young children need much explicit grammatical vocabulary. Most of what they do need can be picked up in context, either through shared reading – discussing how authors have achieved their effects – or by games and activities that focus on specific concepts and provide an opportunity to use grammatical vocabulary as part of the deal. In Shared Writing, the teacher can then demonstrate how grammatical knowledge is applied during the act of composition.

What is a sentence?

As all teachers know, it's extremely difficult to define a sentence. One reason for this is that sentences are not important in spoken language, which tends to be quite disorganised, fragmented and interspersed with time-fillers such as 'like', 'sort of' and 'errrm'. Children, therefore, need to know that in writing, ideas must be more carefully organised.

We can start introducing children to written language patterns as soon as possible by ensuring that they **hear** lots of written language – every time we read to children we are giving them experience of carefully constructed sentences. We can also take every opportunity, in shared reading and writing, to **demonstrate** what sentences are and **talk about** how they help texts make sense, for instance:

- by highlighting or writing each sentence of a text in a different colour;
- by asking pupils to read a familiar text round a group, one sentence each;
- by giving the gist of a sentence from a book in oral 'note form' and asking pupils to identify and read the 'complete sentence'.

During short sentence level teaching sessions, we can **show how sentences are made** using concrete materials, e.g. words and phrases written on cards, held by children to create human sentences, or arranged on a washing line, velcro strip or other sequencing device.

Filling in the detail

When we're speaking, we're usually in the same place as our audience, and we usually know something about them. This means we can take a lot for granted. We can make assumptions about shared knowledge, let background detail go through 'on the nod', impart information by gesture and tone of voice.

Young children's spoken language is particularly implicit. They assume their audience knows what they're talking about and, since their vocabulary is as yet undeveloped, they seldom provide much detail. We can help develop an eye (and ear) for detail by activities such as:

- providing interesting artefacts to talk about and collecting words about them;
- playing 'talking games', e.g. one child describes a picture that his/her friends cannot see;
- asking children to draw a picture of something they've done, then talking about it, drawing out detail of what everything looked like, where and when it happened, what it felt like;
- putting up a poster with the words *Who? What? When? Where? How? What were your feelings?* as an aide memoire to remind pupils of the importance of background detail during class talk;
- using drama, role-play and puppetry to enhance children's awareness of background detail through experience.

Types of sentences

In speech, there isn't time to think very carefully about the way we organise our words. We tend to state what happened fairly baldly, and then add any necessary detail afterwards. In writing this can seem terribly repetitive, so good writers use a variety of sentence structures, to maintain their readers' interest. This involves varying:

- sentence length – some long sentences, some short ones;
- sentence type – occasional use of questions or exclamations;
- word order, e.g. in these sentences, the phrases given in bold (which answer the questions *how? when?* and *where?*, can all be moved around to create different emphases and effects:

> ***Last night*** */ the dog howled /* ***slowly and sadly*** */* ***in the back garden.***
>
> *The baby gurgled /* ***happily*** */* ***for hours*** */* ***in his cot****.*

In shared reading, we can draw attention to how authors vary sentence length by using highlighter pens or tape. In Shared Writing, we can demonstrate how to use questions or exclamations to add interest, e.g.:

What was she to do? *What a surprise!*

We can also build up awareness of sentence variety during short sentence level lessons, e.g.:

- by giving a basic sentence such as *The children waited* or *The ghost wailed* for children to improve by answering the questions *How? When? Where?*
- by using human sentences or words and phrases on a washing line, to show how you can move the *How? When?* and *Where?* chunks around, to improve the sound of your sentence.

Joined-up thinking

As children develop greater control over language, they are ready to express increasingly complex ideas. Longer stories, for instance, usually involve a sequence of events. In spoken language, sequence is shown very simply by the linking words *and then … and then … and then …* In written language this sounds repetitive and boring, so children need to build up a repertoire of time connectives (e.g. see 'Recount case study 2').

As time goes on, they will be ready to express other relationships between ideas, such as cause and effect or conditionality. To do this effectively in writing, they need to construct complex sentences, linking their ideas with conjunctions such as *because*, *although*, *unless* and *until*. Children need opportunities to meet these words in context and to practise using them to link their own ideas – speaking frames (as illustrated in the 'Explanation' section on page 63) are useful for this.

As well as using complex sentences, children will begin to write longer and longer texts. These texts must be 'cohesive' – that is, they must hold together, making complete sense to the reader. One important aspect of cohesion is consistency – if a piece of writing starts in the past tense, it shouldn't drift into the present; if it starts in the first person (*I*), it shouldn't drift into a third person account (*he* or *she*).

In Shared Writing you can demonstrate how to repeatedly and cumulatively re-read your work, checking that it makes sense and 'sounds right'. A poster like the one on page 14 can be used to encourage children to do this too.

Longer texts also need **sentence connectives** – words which make links **between** sentences in the same way that conjunctions make links between clauses. We've already mentioned sequential connectives (like *next* and *then*). Some more able children may begin to use logical connectives such as *however* and *therefore.*

And ... But ... Or ... So ...

A common problem mentioned by teachers is that children often want to start sentences with the words *and, but, or* or *so.* Technically speaking, these are coordinating conjunctions which should always occur in the middle of a sentence, linking two clauses. In written language, they shouldn't be used to start a sentence. However, when writing informally (e.g. when writing for children), authors often mirror spoken language patterns, and thus begin sentences with *And … But … Or … So …* (I do it all the time.) Children therefore see plenty of examples of this usage, and want to copy it.

With young children, the only answer is to explain that grown-up authors are sometimes allowed to break the rules, but when we're first learning to write we must stick to them, to make sure we know the 'correct' way of writing. However, as children become more aware of language, you could put up a poster showing some formal equivalents of *and, but, or* and *so:*

And – Also	*So – Therefore*
But – However	*Or – On the other hand*

If children want to start a sentence with one of the coordinating conjunctions, they can see whether the formal word would do instead.

Punctuation

As pupils write at greater length, they need increasing control over punctuation.

In spoken language we can use our voices to make meaning clear – conveying where one 'chunk of meaning' ends and another begins by tiny pauses or by changes in tone or pitch. In written language, the only substitute for the voice is a system of dots, dashes and squiggles which mean very little to children.

It's therefore very important to take every opportunity to draw attention to punctuation and how it affects how we read. The main functions of punctuation relevant in the early stages of writing are:

- it conveys grammatical boundaries, helping to make meaning clear (capitalisation for the first word of a sentence, full stop, comma, dash);
- it can convey tone of voice (as for a question or exclamation);
- in narrative, it clarifies which text is direct speech and which is not (speech marks).

There are many ways of drawing attention to punctuation marks during sentence level sessions, such as:

- asking children to highlight certain punctuation marks in colour on a shared text;
- inventing actions for 'physical punctuation' (e.g. drawing the shape in the air) and punctuating sentences as you read or say them;
- inventing sounds for each mark, which children can make as you read a text aloud.

Standard English

Many children come to school speaking a regional or ethnic dialect of English, rather than the standard version in which they learn to read and write. If we suggest this non-standard English is somehow 'wrong' or 'inferior', we could offend both the children and their parents. It's therefore important to be clear about what standard English is, and why we teach it.

Standard English has its roots in the dialect spoken 500 years ago in the south east of England, at the time of the first printing presses. This dialect became the form of language in which our written heritage – literature and learning – was encoded, as well as the dialect of our institutions (government, the law, education). All children therefore have a right to know their 'national dialect' as well as any home dialect. Without it they'd be disadvantaged in formal social situations, and would have difficulty expressing themselves in writing.

Standard English may be spoken in any accent. It differs from dialect forms in terms of vocabulary and grammar. But other dialect grammars are just as valid in other social contexts. In a dialect-speaking home, it would be just as correct to say 'we was going on us holidays', as it would to write 'We were going on our holidays' in school. Dialect grammars are *non-standard*, **not** sub-standard.

Dialect grammar is different in different parts of the country. It can help to keep a note of any non-standard forms used by children in the class. You can then draw attention to these forms and their standard equivalents when the topic arises (without drawing attention to particular children's usage). When a child speaks to you in non-standard English, the best response is to repeat the words **in a natural voice**, adjusting it to standard. Teachers should also always provide a model of standard English usage in their own speech.

Appendix 2 Shared, Guided and Independent Writing

The point of 'nuts and bolts' teaching is to provide children with sub-skills that help them explore and express their ideas in a written form. So teaching must always ultimately be about the construction of whole texts – as soon as the teaching of writing begins, Shared, Guided and Independent Writing become the vehicles for whole text work.

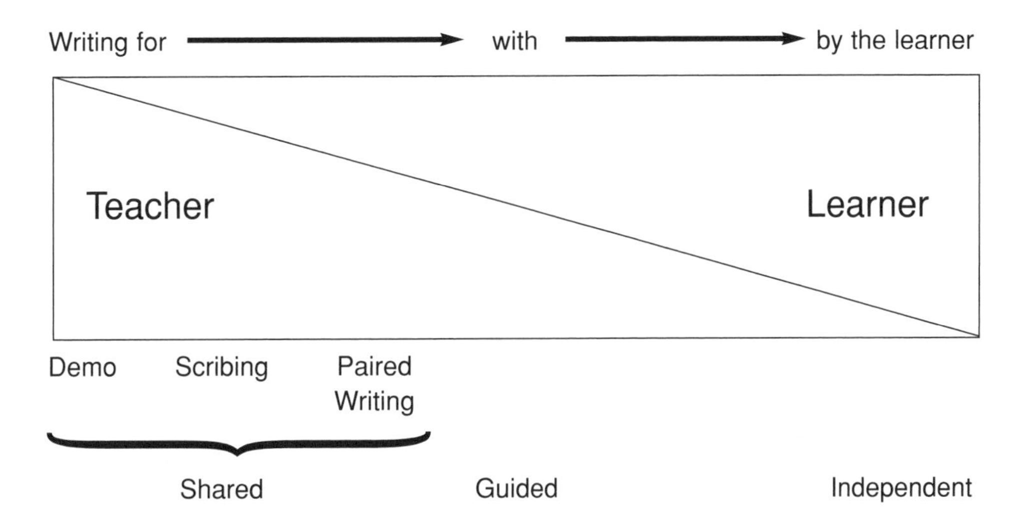

Figure A2.1 Varying levels of support

Between them, Shared, Guided and Independent Writing provide for many different levels of support. At the start, the teacher takes complete control. S/he then gradually hands it over to the children so that, during Independent Writing, they are empowered to write for themselves.

In the early stages, while children are acquiring basic phonic and handwriting skills, the distinction between the three types of teaching is often blurred:

- most young children need individual attention when attempting to write, either from the teacher or from classroom helpers, so until formal teaching begins this is usually on an ad hoc basis;
- as time goes on, groups of children of roughly similar ability should emerge, who would benefit from short group sessions;
- these first groupings benefit most from small-scale Shared Writing sessions as described in the chart above.

As the children mature, the number of participants in Shared Writing sessions is likely to swell until, by the time they're seven or eight, the whole class can join in. At this point, the teacher will also need to identify smaller Guided Writing groups (about six children of roughly similar ability) with whom to concentrate on specific aspects of writing at their own level.

Shared Writing

The technique of Shared Writing is a way of demonstrating to children how word and sentence level sub-skills are brought together in the act of writing. The recording of information learned across the curriculum provides an ideal context for illustrating this 'orchestration' of writing skills. There are three ways to approach it:

Table A2.1 Techniques for Shared Writing

Demonstration	Scribing	Supported Writing
The teacher models the process of writing for the children. The teacher writes a section of text on the board or flip-chart, and keeps up a constant commentary on what s/he is doing and why. This could include explicit demonstration of recently covered topics, such as how to segment and blend words to write them phonetically. This demonstrates to children exactly how ideas get out of someone's head and onto the page. It also demonstrates exactly what the child should be doing and thinking when trying to write independently.	Scribing is a way of involving the class in the composition of Shared Writing. The teacher invites them to contribute ideas, forms of words, alternative constructions, etc.. Children should be given the opportunity to talk with a partner for a few seconds, to discuss and choose the best word, phrase or sentence. The teacher chooses one of their offerings and says why s/he likes it. This form of words is integrated into the demonstration, with the teacher still keeping up the commentary.	Every so often, the teacher asks pairs of pupils to work on a section of text together. The best Supported Writing tasks involve putting one or more of the day's learning objectives into immediate practice. It is helpful to display a visual reminder of an agreed procedure for Supported Writing (e.g. see page 14). Otherwise valuable time can be lost reminding pupils orally, and this interferes with their auditory memory of the specific writing task. When pupils give feedback, the procedure continues as for 'Scribing'.

Guided Writing

After the highly directed experience of Shared Writing, children need opportunities to try out the process for themselves, writing independently or with a degree of teacher supervision. Bringing children together in Guided Writing groups (of roughly similar ability) allows the teacher to home in more closely on specific children's needs than is possible in the Shared session. There are three major advantages to working with Guided Writing groups rather than with individual children.

- In a group situation, there is less temptation to focus too heavily on a particular child and thus offer more support or direction than is helpful. Too much 'help' can make children over-dependent on adult intervention. Within a group, the teacher can focus in general on the teaching objective, rather than any individual child.
- While it is obviously helpful to offer selective prompting about basic skills at point of need – at the very moment when children are writing – it is difficult to achieve a sensitive balance between:
  - guiding children towards correctness;
  - encouraging them to think for themselves and 'take risks' in their writing.
- Over-emphasis on correctness is more likely to inhibit writing development than to aid it. In a group it is easier to point out errors in a more general way, without directing the spotlight at any one individual.
- Children benefit infinitely more from praise for what they achieve than from having attention drawn to their mistakes. In a group, the teacher can single out individual pupils for praise and thus, incidentally, raise awareness among all group members about what is deserving of praise.

While Guided Writing groups are usually pretty constant, it may sometimes be more appropriate occasionally to form 'ad hoc' groups, to tackle particular aspects of writing. If the majority of an ability group is secure on, say, capital letters for proper names, it would be wasteful to make that the focus of an entire session for them. When a writing task arises that provides a good vehicle for re-teaching the topic, the teacher can create a one-off group of children from across the class who need help with that aspect of sentence level work.

Independent Writing

As children develop as writers, they need more and more opportunities to write independently, without adult intervention. By the time they're seven or eight, it should be possible in most classrooms to arrange at least two sessions (of about 20 minutes) per week specifically dedicated to Independent Writing, during which the teacher works with a Guided Writing group. Such sessions will generally follow directly after a Shared Writing session, so that children have watched the teacher model the relevant writing behaviour before going off to try it for themselves. As time goes on, there will be many further occasions, throughout the curriculum, when children have opportunities to write independently.

Independent Writing is their opportunity to put all the nuts and bolts they've been learning into practice. But most children need the structure of:

- well-established classroom procedures for obvious problems like checking on a spelling (see Appendix 1, page 81) – children should be well-trained in these procedures and should not need to keep checking with the teacher;
- classroom organisation that avoids obvious 'flashpoints'; for instance, it is often better if easily distracted children do not sit together, which may mean that members of the less able group are spread among their peers for independent work;
- knowing exactly what they are expected to do, and what the teacher is looking for; objectives and outcomes should be clearly described (the less able the child, the more specific should be the expected outcomes).

It's often enlightening to spend a day or two every so often observing independent work, rather than taking a group. If children are told that the teacher is still out of bounds on these occasions, they soon forget they are being watched, and one can learn much about classroom culture. On the basis of playing 'the invisible teacher', it may be possible to make adjustments to the organisation of furniture, equipment and so on that will lead to calmer behaviour. The teacher can also use his/her observations as the basis of a discussion with the class to negotiate classroom rules and procedures – children with 'ownership' of the rules are usually more interested in keeping them.

It goes without saying that teachers should be aware of each child's potential, and on the whole, response to errors in Independent Writing should be to ask oneself what further teaching is required (or, more likely, what revision of previous teaching). As time goes on, however, some children's development – particularly in terms of phonic and/or handwriting skills – lags behind that of their peers.

It's therefore very important to identify slow developers as early as possible, try to work out the reason behind their difficulties, and provide appropriate 'catch-up' support. This requires the involvement of the Special Needs Coordinator and is outwith the scope of this book. On a day-to-day level, however, teachers should always try to ensure that during Independent Writing, provision is made to support such children through specific areas of difficulty, for instance by providing a spelling mat (see pages 82–83). And whenever they get something right, praise them!

This type of specific support is sometimes referred to as 'scaffolding', so that each child is able to engage with a writing task in a way that ensures active mental processing at a level likely to encourage learning. 'Scaffolding out' each individual's problems is considerably easier said than done, but worth pursuing. Empowering children to write for themselves – at whatever level is appropriate for the individual learner – is the most likely way of helping them become enthusiastic and successful writers in the long run.

Appendix 3 Case study materials

Tom Bowker's Eve

Long long ago, on a stormy winter's night, one man saved a whole town from starvation. This is the story of Tom Bowker, who braved the storms to snatch food from the sea.

In the far south-west of England, the county of Cornwall sticks out like a foot into the Atlantic Ocean. Near the very tip of Cornwall's toe is the little town of Mousehole, (or 'Mowsul' as the Cornish people say it). It got its name from the way fishing boats ventured out from the harbour into stormy seas, then scurried back like mice into their hole, bringing fish for the townsfolk to eat.

Then one year the storms were so bad that no boats dared leave the shelter of the harbour walls. Huge waves lashed the quayside, and people cowered in their houses, growing hungrier and hungrier. As Christmas drew near, children sobbed for want of food, starvation stalked the town, and still the storms raged.

At last, on 23rd December, Tom Bowker battled through the rain to his fishing boat. Other men volunteered to go with him, but he turned them away: they had families, while Tom had none. As dusk fell, there was a lull in the storm ... and Tom cast off into the dark seas, throwing his nets into the waves. Then the storm swelled again, and the people of Mousehole, praying for his safe return, put lamps in their windows to light him back.

By some miracle, Tom's boat survived. The lights guided him home and the villagers rushed to help drag his catch up on to the quay. They made a special pie that night, a pie of many fishes, and named it Star-Gazy Pie after the lights that had twinkled all over Mousehole. And the townsfolk gave thanks for the hero who had saved them from starvation.

Now, every 23rd December Mousehole celebrates Tom Bowker's Eve. The town and harbour are festooned with lights, and everyone goes down to the Ship Inn on the quay, for a special meal of Star-Gazy Pie.

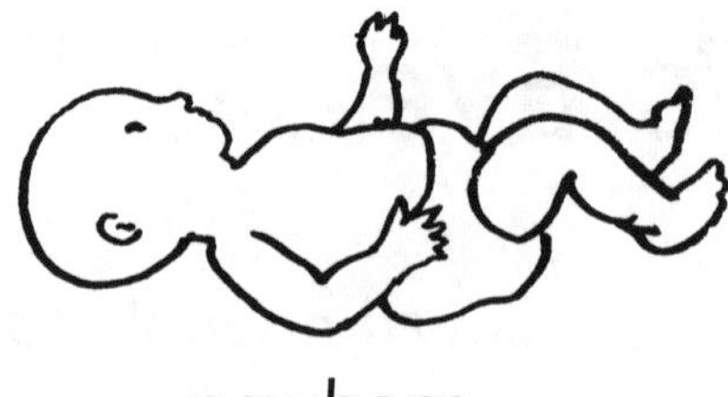

newborn

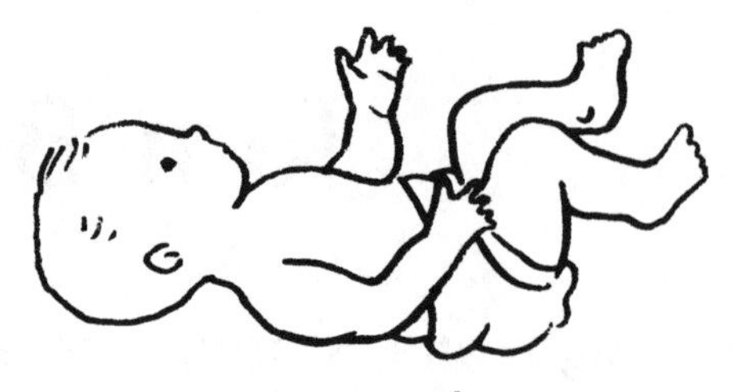

six weeks

three months

six months

one year

two years

	Newborn	6 weeks	3 months	6 months	1 year	2 years
Average weight	$3\frac{1}{2}$ kg	4 kg	6 kg	8 kg	$9\frac{1}{2}$ kg	13 kg
Average height	53 cm	55 cm	60 cm	68 cm	72 cm	86 cm